Coping Alone

Coping Alone
was first published by Arlen House in 1982

This completely revised and updated edition 1990 by
Poolbeg Press Ltd.
Knocksedan House,
Swords, Co. Dublin, Ireland.

© 1990 Clara Clark

ISBN 1 85371 095 4

Cover design by Pomphrey Associates
Typeset by Typeform Ltd.
Printed by The Guernsey Press Ltd.,
Vale, Guernsey, Channel Islands.

Coping Alone

A Handbook for Single Parents

Clara Clark

POOLBEG

ACKNOWLEDGEMENTS

My thanks to Philip MacDermott of Poolbeg Press for provoking me into producing this updated edition, and to my two editors, Jo O'Donoghue and Angela Rohan, who were painstaking and thorough, despite my best attempts to cut corners.

I am indebted to Mairead Foley and her colleagues in the Information Section of the Department of social welfare, who guided me through the very new social welfare provisions for lone parents; and to Mairead Leyne, who checked the legal sections for accuracy. My thanks also to Barbara Wood of Gingerbread and Tony Grant, whose insights into single parents and the hurdles facing second relationships helped enormously.

Sincere thanks to all my colleagues in AIM Group, for their time, their literature, their expertise and their continuing help and support to people in marital discord and distress. AIM is a very professional voluntary organisation. To my now-grown children, Simon and Frances, for so successfully surviving my single parenting.

Finally, my appreciation and thanks to Charles Mollan, whose active support and encouragement made possible the task of writing, alongside a family and a demanding job. I am also indebted to him for the use of his computer hardware and software, his sharing of time and space in the midst of his own publications, and his valuable suggestions and amendments. All remaining mistakes are my own.

Clara Clark
June 1990

To Charles and Luke, the light at the end of my tunnel

CONTENTS

Introduction

This is a "how to" book; not a "how to mend the plumbing, shampoo the dog and the carpet in thirty minutes" book, but a "how to stay cheerful, sane and hopeful" book for when the world looks cheerless and hostile and you are in despair. In short, it tells you how to cope as a single parent.

Single parents can be widows, widowers, unmarried mothers or fathers, deserted, separated or divorced parents, prisoners' spouses—anyone rearing children single-handed. Throughout I refer to lone or "single" parents but at no time is this a reference to marital status. The importance of this point was brought home to me while listening to a radio programme on the subject, when an irate widow telephoned in to say that she was not a single parent, she was respectably widowed. I make no such distinctions: lone parents are single parents.

I write this as one who has lived alone, rearing children, and knows what it is to be ill with no one to take over, untrained for any job other than motherhood, broke, jobless and a social oddity. Ten years of living alone after my marriage ended provided me with all the

1

experience I needed. There are no magic formulas for learning to cope, no instant or easy solutions. How each person manages will depend not only on the individual situation but on the personality of the person concerned. What works for one person may not work for another; what suits me would probably drive you crazy. Realise and accept that there will be bad times and problems; but being able to see beyond these is what coping is about.

I write this book from a woman's point of view, but many of the situations and most of the problems will be faced by men in similar circumstances, who are rearing children and coping alone. Much of the information will be of particular relevance to those who have been married, so unmarried parents will have to bear with me if the book appears to lean rather heavily in that direction. However, this book is a guide and, I hope, a help for all lone parents, married or not.

This is a new and completely updated edition of a book first published in 1982. Sadly, the need for it is greater now than ever. There are far more lone parents, particularly separated and single mothers, than before. In the intervening years, I have had many requests for my book and it is in response to these that this edition of *Coping Alone* has been produced.

1

Learning to Cope

Memories, like newspaper cuttings and old photographs, fade with time and lose their relevance if not their poignancy. Time kaleidoscopes; the rough patches drop out of sight and the new horizon builds up into a vibrant pattern.

Great, you say, but when? From where you're sitting it's all black, bleak and terrible. Your husband/wife/partner has died/walked out/gone to prison; your parents have just died/emigrated. For whatever reason, you are suddenly left alone and the world you have known and lived in has just crumbled into a pile of rubble at your feet. How do you begin? Where do you start? How do you gather the courage and strength to pick yourself up and start again? As Robert Browning said: "To dry one's eyes and laugh at a fall,/and baffled, get up and begin again."

Baffled, however, is an understatement! Even stunned, shattered, wrecked, ill, cannot really describe feelings that blot out the will to live, to face another day or hour in complete despair. Years ago, when I felt this hopeless and desperate, I used to write snatches of poetry to try to express and ease the hurt. One of these ran:

Time standing still, and marching on.
In isolation searching in expectation for
    inspiration
And a meaning.
Reasoning is exhausted. Struggling for
    objectivity
In emotional turmoil.

Two months later I took a deep breath and walked out of a five-year-old, violent, unhappy marriage, taking my two very small children and whatever belongings I could fit into a borrowed car. I was twenty-two years old. I can vividly recall my one overwhelming fear: not that I had no home, no job, no money, no family support, no prospects, but the fact that I knew no one at all in a similar situation. I felt that I totally lacked identity; I stood alone and didn't belong.

For so many it is this crippling fear, of being alone and different, that binds us to intolerable situations. And leaving is a frightening step. It is so much easier, more sensible perhaps (in society's eyes), to hide behind the façade of a marriage or to bury your life in the children or a few little drinks when everyone is out. It can be more acceptable, too, to put on a brave face and get some little pills from the doctor when the going gets rough. Stepping outside to face the world alone is a daunting prospect for many reasons, but can also be very rewarding and satisfying.

Some of the Initial Problems

Education has not prepared women to cope alone. Implicit in most textbooks and attitudes is the presumption that there will be bank managers, insurance brokers, doctors, dentists, lawyers, plumbers and politicians to consult about whatever problems we may have. The fact that, to date, these people have predominantly been male has left us seeing these male omnipotents making our decisions for us, organising our finances, our reproductive patterns, our lives. Professional help should always be availed of, but you should remain in control yourself. Do not abdicate responsibility for these issues by handing over the decision-making to someone else.

How many wives, for instance, do not know how to pay bills or fill in tax and insurance forms, how much heating fuel or the TV licence costs, or what the car insurance cover is? It may be possible to go through life unconcerned about such details, presuming husband and money remain at hand. But there is the catch. What happens if one or both disappear? Whatever about your hopes of growing old together, the fact is some husbands do die in their forties and fifties, sometimes younger; and an increasing number of marriages break up. Women are being left to cope on their own with families and mortgages, hire purchase payments and homes to be cared for, paid for and run.

My own convent boarding-school taught embroidery, Gregorian chant and Italian, but we were allowed to drop mathematics after the intermediate examination. There was no suggestion at that time that it would be useful to be numerate if one were to hold down a job, much less run a household. I do remember that commercial courses were recommended for girls who were not very bright—perhaps it was assumed that the bright ones would use their brains to catch rich husbands who would rescue them from the ignominy of toil.

5

The fact is that until our system of education drops sex-typing and places as much emphasis on educating boys and girls as competent, confident individuals, equally able to cook, mend a fuse, sew in a zip and balance a budget, as it does on the academic and technical subjects, we are not going to change anything radically. Nor do I speak only of schools. Sex discrimination begins in the home and it is taught at a much earlier age, when a child is very receptive to attitudes and impressions. So it is that sons go fishing or mow the lawn with fathers while daughters help mothers with the domestic chores. How many teenage boys do their own ironing?

There are emotional dangers too. Girls are kissed and cosseted in childhood when they hurt themselves, in contrast to boys who must brave it out "like men"; the boys may then grow up too anxious to express emotion other than through violence. Having suppressed their gentler feelings in youth, men are often unable to demonstrate even the most basic feelings like joy, sorrow, hurt, defeat; unable sometimes to show love and affection to their own wives and children. If our teenagers are unable to talk naturally to each other, is it really so surprising? They are doing, after all, exactly as they have been taught. So many wives turn to other women, even total strangers (while men may turn either to other women or to drink), to talk over issues and problems which should be discussed between husband and wife, that it seems the communication bridge in some relationships is never crossed; even during the turmoils of courtship, marriage and parenthood. Couples seem to be sharing so much and yet so little.

Whatever children learn from us about expressing feelings, it does not follow that we are responsible for

6

everything they do. Lone parents, more than most, tend to assume blame for everything that goes wrong where their children are concerned. I worried terribly and blamed myself, and the fact that I had chosen to go it alone, for countless behavioural traits that my children developed, including clinging, bed-wetting, sulkiness with visitors and so on. I visited child psychologists, told my doctor, spent sleepless nights worrying and feeling guilty, until gradually it dawned that most families have one or more children who go through at least one of these problems and these children often come from secure, stable two-parent families. Ultimately the problems may crop up whether there are two of you or one.

If you wish to look into the whole area of how children cope with divorce and marital break-up, two very interesting books are *Surviving the Breakup—How Children and Parents Cope with Divorce* by Judith Wallerstein and Joan Berlin Kelly, and *Second Chances—Men, Women and Children a Decade after Divorce* by Judith Wallerstein and Sandra Blakeslee (see Appendix Two, page 226). These books follow a number of American families through the ten years following their divorces and make in-depth studies of how each child and parent in each family reacts and adjusts as the years go by. Your teenage children would also find them helpful. They are certainly worth reading if you are about to embark on a second relationship or marriage.

Stigmas

Society is changing. Gradually it is becoming more accepting and more understanding of deserted wives, separated and divorced people, widows and women who choose to remain single. The old stigma attached to being unmarried over the age of thirty is dying and the attitude that all widows, unmarried mothers, separated and deserted women, irrespective of age, should bury themselves or live like hermits is also fading, and not before time.

But Ireland, like most places, is still very much a couple-orientated society and women on their own do not generally get invited out in mixed company. Instead, single women may be invited when the husband is away or working but not for a party or dinner with husbands present. It is as though one's status drops and, while it is okay to come with the kids for coffee, you cannot expect to be asked on your own to a party. Yet, because most newly "single" women have children and spend most of their time with children or on their own, the prospect of some mixed adult company over drinks or a meal, or just being in surroundings other than one's own, would be a treat very much appreciated.

There seem to be several problems invloved, not least being the obligation which some hosts feel to provide you with an escort, whether you want one or not—a gesture I sometimes think is motivated more by self-preservation than kindness. It is not entirely unconnected to the prevailing attitude which depicts unattached women as loose or sex-starved, and husbands as potential, and of course innocent, victims. Wives may not want to admit it, but the fact is that their husbands do, occasionally, make the running; although in this uncharted behavioural minefield I suspect men do so more because they feel they should than out of simple vanity.

It works both ways. Women make passes at newly "single" men. Either way, sexual overtures are not always welcome. Lone parents suffer the same shattering feelings of loss and disorientation as a bereaved person, and emotionally they may be unable to cope. Later will be the time for exploring the new sexual territory and your new sexual inclinations. For now, you might prefer to enjoy the company of the opposite sex without the competitive pressure of being pursued. In any case, social boundaries may be restricted by children and a lack of money and free time; this is a time for the support of family and friends, if possible.

You will probably find that when you become single again, having been part of a couple, your friends change or simply melt away. This is particularly true of former mutual friends who may not know how to handle the situation now that you are alone. Whatever the reason, you will be hurt; especially when you are so much in need of moral support and friendship and find that friends no longer ring, call or include you in social gatherings. This is the time when you most need someone to talk to and a few hours away from the pressures of trying to cope. If only, you think, someone would come and take the children off your hands for a couple of hours so that you could go to bed for a rest, go shopping, get your hair done, take a walk alone or have a night out. It would be such a break. Couples take such simple respites from responsibility so much for granted that they do not think to offer to help you. Most people left suddenly on their own need breathing-space, time to think, reorganise their lives and decide where they are going from here.

Loneliness

For most single parents or separated people aloneness is a fact of life, an inevitable part of being outside the social norm. This is not to say that all single parents are lonely. However, the experience of aloneness is something which can create additional difficulties when you are faced with ill-health, decision-making or even Christmas, since these are problems or events which most people share with others.

A single parent—single for whatever reason—does not belong to either marital status group. One is neither fancy-free and single (as the myth goes) nor married. He or she is, on the one hand, tied by children and without the time, money or perhaps even the inclination to seek out a social life, while on the other hand lacking the companionship of caring adult company in family life.

Usually the loss is a sudden one. All at once the bereaved, the separated or deserted, the recently delivered single mother, the woman whose husband has just gone to prison, is thrust into a social limbo. Friends are equally thrown: few know quite how to react or what to say. Most are embarrassed or shocked; they feel sorry for you and cope with their confusion by pretending that the problem (you) does not exist. Under these pressures you may be tempted to think of yourself as a half-person or your family as a half-family. This is a mistake. You and your spouse may have been a couple but now you are the head of the household (whether or not you have a house) and you and the children remain a family.

This may seem so obvious that it needs no saying. But many, many people left to cope with a family do not feel like one and continue to think there is a part missing. If, however, that part has gone, then the sooner you can adjust your thinking to the fact that what is left is still a family, the better. After all, unless you see yourselves as a complete family—even if it is one that is slightly reduced in number, you cannot expect others to either. Friends, officialdom and ultimately society will accept you as a family all the sooner if you do. Of course, there will be exceptions. Old notions about family life die hard, and new, although hardly radical, ideas about single parenting and alternative (to marriage, that is) families are not universally accepted. However, if you are unapologetic about your new status you will elicit respect rather than misplaced sympathy or hostility.

The 1986 Census recorded 81,087 households consisting solely of a lone parent with children. Eighty-two per cent of these households were headed by women. However, a special analysis of this Census revealed 85,693 mothers who were not living with a man: 64 per cent of these were widowed, 17 per cent married, 11 per cent separated and 7 per cent single. Between them, these women had over 160,000 children or, on average, two children each. (From *Women and Poverty* by Mary Daly—see Appendix Two page 226.) You are not alone.

Every year the Samaritans receive hundreds of calls from people who are lonely, depressed, in despair, suicidal. An increasing number of these calls come from single parents emotionally crushed by the pressures of trying to cope. The most common problem appears to be the terrible, crippling loneliness of a parent tied to the house by children, with no money, no social life and little contact with the outside world. Stresses like these can lead to child-battering, drinking to blot out the problems and a horrific fear of cracking up with the children being taken into care.

If you feel depressed or desperate and cannot tell neighbours or friends, ring or call the Samaritans, day or night. They are glad to listen to all who telephone or call in and no problem is too small to merit their attention. Their service is totally confidential and you do not need to give your name or any personal details which could identify you. They have branches in Dublin, Cork, Galway, Limerick and Waterford. (See Appendix One or the phone book for telephone numbers.)

Marriage Counselling

Marriage counselling agencies do not deal exclusively with continuing marriages. Their counsellors are trained, ready to listen and do not view marriage as "togetherness at any price." If, in the aftermath of your marriage, you feel the need of professional, unbiased help with the problems of adjustment, marriage counselling may have something to offer. The addresses of these agencies and other counselling agencies are in Appendix One. It is usually necessary to make an appointment.

You Need Friends

Friends are important. It could be damaging to your health, physical and mental, to shut yourself away and suffer silently. If you have children it is your responsibility to keep up some sort of social contact. Mixing is essential to give everyone a balanced outlook and children should have the chance to interact with other children and adults. When a child has lost a parent, for whatever reason, she must be given the opportunity to mix with adults of the same sex as the missing parent. Only in this way can the child identify with that other; seeing that dads are different from mums and not just physically and how men and women relate to each other in two-parent situations or simply as friends. Quite apart from anything else, children should see that, while their parents' marriage did not last, it is possible for some mums and dads to have good, happy, loving relationships with each other. This may mean finding new friends in your new role. If the idea fills you with terror, find someone in a similar situation to yourself, either through acquaintances, neighbours, or by contacting an appropriate organisation like the National Association of Widows, Cherish, Gingerbread or some of the other "singles" groups. (See Appendix One for addresses and telephone numbers.)

The advantage of approaching a group is that they hold meetings regularly and run socials where new faces are welcomed. You do not have to answer any personal questions about yourself if you do not want to, but you can draw on other people's ideas and share some of the practical problems like baby-sitting, house-sharing, holiday-sharing, or discuss practical difficulties like those of raising children single-handed.

Some people find it reassuring to discover that the worries/problems/feelings they have are not peculiar to them but are similar to those experienced by countless others; that one is not unique in feeling lonely, abandoned, empty, bitter, frustrated, distraught or just plain exhausted. In fact, the Wallerstein study of families a decade after divorce, *Second Chances* (see Appendix Two), discovered that these feelings lasted for many years at high intensity rather than diminishing as one might expect (and hope!). Your adjustment will depend on your personality and your circumstances, and on your ability to rise above the past.

While many people enjoy the feeling of solidarity and support which self-help groups offer, several warn against the dangers of identifying too much with your group and its members. They point out that it is potentially isolating, not so much for oneself but for children, who may grow up in an environment which is exclusively one-parent-oriented. In short, make the most of the organisations that are there to help you get back on your feet, availing of the support, encouragement and practical advice, but view these as stepping-stones towards your future independence when you will re-enter the mainstream of society, albeit with a new identity.

In any case, children do not like to be different. They feel the need to belong, to be part of what their friends and class-mates are; they want to wear similar clothes, do similar things, have parties, treats and a life-style similar to that of their peers. Initially you will probably not be able to come up with everything they want. The struggle to keep yourselves housed and fed may absorb every minute of your time and energy. But in looking ahead your aim must be not merely to survive, but to have fun doing family things, growing and learning as all families do.

2

Making Ends Meet

One of the first and most pressing problems facing the lone parent will probably be money, or the lack of it. Whether or not it is a cause of marital disharmony, it is certainly the cause of a lot of worry for many parents left to cope alone.

For this reason, money, including social welfare benefits, pensions, medical cards, maintenance, finding work, and other related topics, is dealt with first. Each subject is given a separate heading to make it easier for the reader to find the relevant section. It is designed as a guide to be referred to as the need arises.

Social Welfare

Various social welfare entitlements are listed below. That which applies to you depends on your situation, so look under the headings which follow. More information on any of these can be obtained from the Department of Social Welfare, College Road, Sligo. Unless otherwise stated in the text, queries on the payments mentioned are dealt with from this address. The Department publishes a *Guide to Social Welfare Services* which is available free, if you ask. You can request information by writing to the above address or by calling to your local social welfare information office or community information centre. These are listed in the *Guide* booklet.

Lone Parent's Allowance

The Social Welfare Act, 1990, has made a number of important changes relating to the means-tested allowances payable to lone parents. It has introduced a Lone Parent's Allowance for anyone looking after children on their own which replaces the Unmarried Mother's Allowance, the Widower's Non-Contributory Pension, the Deserted Husband's Allowance and the Prisoner's Wife's Allowance. This new allowance is extended to separated spouses who did not qualify for Deserted Wife's or Deserted Husband's Allowance under the old arrangements, and to unmarried fathers and prisoners' husbands. There is a single means test for all these categories of people, broadly similar to that for unmarried mother's allowance. The old Widow's Non-Contributory Pension, the Deserted Wife's Allowance and the Prisoner's Wife's Allowance will remain in place for women without children. The Widow's Contributory Pension and the Deserted Wife's Benefit, which are non-means-tested and paid on the basis of PRSI contributions, will remain unchanged.

There are two main types of social welfare payments:

(1) **benefit** payments are based on the number of pay-related social insurance contributions (PRSI) which you or your spouse have paid while in employment. If you or your spouse have made no contributions or have

insufficient to qualify for benefit, then you will probably qualify for (2) **allowance** payments, provided you satisfy a means test. Your entitlement depends on your particular circumstances. If you are not sure to which category you belong, ask the Department of Social Welfare.

Desertion, Separation and Divorce

There is a benefit payment for deserted wives, but no equivalent payment for deserted husbands. The means-tested Lone Parent's Allowance is applicable to qualified deserted, separated and divorced wives and husbands (see above). In order to qualify, you must have at least one dependent child living with you.

If you have been deserted by your husband, you can apply for either a Deserted Wife's Benefit or a Lone Parent's Allowance payable to those who do not qualify for the benefit payment.

At present to qualify for **Deserted Wife's Benefit:**

■ you have to be deserted for three months before you can apply, and must prove that you have made reasonable efforts to contact your husband to get him to maintain you. You can apply for Supplementary Welfare Allowance in the interim
and

■ you must have at least one dependent child living with you if you are under forty (a dependent child is any child under eighteen years, or twenty-one years if still receiving full-time education). If you are over forty you do not have to have a child dependent
and

17

- you are not receiving adequate maintenance from your husband
  and
- you must not be cohabiting
  and
- you must satisfy the PRSI conditions, based on either your own or your husband's PRSI record.

Deserted Wife's Benefit is payable for as long as you satisfy these conditions. Your Benefit is not affected by any other income you may have from employment or other sources. Payment will stop if you are awarded a social welfare pension. You may choose to continue to receive the Deserted Wife's Benefit instead, if it is to your advantage.

There are additional weekly allowances if you are aged sixty-six or over and living alone or aged eighty or over.

Deserted Wife's Benefit is liable for income tax. The Social Welfare Act, 1990 is phasing out the exemption which lone parents had to the employee portion of PRSI. By 5 April, 1992, lone parents will pay a 5.5 per cent PRSI contribution. If you are receiving Deserted Wife's Benefit you do not have to pay the 1.25 per cent health contribution or the 1 per cent employment and training levy on any of your income.

Lone Parent's Allowance or Deserted Wife's Allowance may be paid if you do not have any or sufficient PRSI contributions to receive the benefit payment.

A Lone Parent's Allowance may be payable if:

- you have been deserted or separated for at least three months and your spouse is not paying adequate maintenance for you or your child/children
  and
- you have made reasonable efforts to get maintenance from him/her
  and
- you have at least one dependent child living with you (if you are under forty)
  and
- you are not cohabiting
  and
- you satisfy a means test.

The Lone Parent's Allowance is paid for as long as you satisfy these conditions.

Changes in your circumstances should be reported to the Department immediately. If you continue to claim an allowance payment for which you cease to be eligible, for example, a Lone Parent's Allowance while you are cohabiting or when your spouse has returned or is providing adequate support, you will be deemed to have been overpaid and be liable to refund the Department of Social Welfare.

The amount of allowance payable depends on the number of dependent children and your weekly means. There are additional allowances for those aged sixty-six and living alone.

Recipients receive butter vouchers and may be eligible for free fuel in winter. You will probably qualify for a medical card but will have to claim separately (see later in this chapter).

You should apply when you have been alone for three months. If you wait longer than six months, you will receive payment only from the date your application is received.

Application forms for Deserted Wife's Benefit and the Lone Parent's Allowance are available from the Department of Social Welfare Pension Services Office, College Road, Sligo or from Information Service, Department of Social Welfare, Store Street, Dublin 1.

If you know of your spouse's whereabouts, you will be expected to seek maintenance from him/her to force a contribution towards your support. You may be refused payment if you fail to make "reasonable efforts" in this area. The Social Welfare Acts, 1989 and 1990, provide for spouses of recipients of Lone Parent's Allowance and Supplementary Welfare Allowance to contribute towards such payments.

If your Spouse is on Social Welfare

While you are on Deserted Wife's Benefit or Lone Parent's Allowance your spouse is not entitled to claim an adult dependent allowance on your behalf; neither may he/she claim any child dependent allowances, unless the children are in his/her care. Child dependent allowances due are included with your benefit or allowance payment.

Income Tax Relief

If you are in taxable employment you should claim the Single Parent Family Allowance. Should you cohabit, you will lose this allowance.

Tracing Your Spouse

If your spouse leaves without notifying you of his/her whereabouts you should contact the local police and report that he/she is missing, even if you can safely assume that he/she has not met with an accident. This will be used for record purposes and helps when you apply for the Deserted Wife's Benefit or the Lone Parent's Allowance. The Salvation Army's Social Services Investigation Department (see Appendix One) will try to have your spouse traced if he/she has left the country. They will not put you in touch if they find him/her but they will ask him/her if he/she is prepared to support you or contribute maintenance in any way. If he/she refuses or cannot be traced, then this can be used as proof that you have tried to get maintenance.

If you are Single and Have a Child

You may qualify for the Lone Parent's Allowance provided:

- ■ you are the parent of at least one dependent child under eighteen years (or twenty-one years if in full-time education)
  and
- ■ you are not cohabiting
  and
- ■ you satisfy a means test.

The payment continues as long as you satisfy the above conditions. Payment stops if you marry or leave the State.

The rate of allowance payable depends on the number of children you have and the extent of your means from various sources. The current rates of payment are available from the Department of Social Welfare. You should claim the allowance within three months of the birth of your baby. If you apply after this time payment can be made only from the date your application is received.

You can earn a certain amount without affecting your payment. An allowance recipient automatically qualifies for a medical card and butter vouchers. You or your children may also qualify for free milk, a fuel allowance in winter, children's footwear and clothing allowance, supplementary welfare payments or reduced differential rent if you live in local authority housing. Ask about these at your local health board office or community information centre.

Application forms are available from the Department of Social Welfare, College Road, Sligo.

Income Tax Relief

If you are in taxable employment you should apply for the Single Parent Family Tax Allowance.

If your Spouse Goes to Prison

If your spouse goes to prison you may qualify for a Lone Parent's Allowance if:

- your spouse has been sentenced to and is serving a sentence of imprisonment for six months or more. If he/she is sentenced for a shorter time it is assumed that your financial needs can be met by Supplementary Welfare

payments (see page 30)
and
- you have at least one dependent child (if you are under forty)
and
- you satisfy a means test.

The allowance should be claimed as soon as possible after your spouse has been sentenced, and not later than three months after the start of his/her sentence.

The amount payable depends on the number of dependent children you have and your means. Additional allowances are payable to those aged sixty-six or over and living alone.

Recipients also qualify for butter vouchers and, possibly, fuel vouchers in winter. You should ask at your local health board office about a medical card, children's footwear and clothing allowance and, if you need it, Supplementary Welfare.

You can earn a certain amount without affecting your payment, which stops four weeks after your spouse is released from prison. Application forms are available from the Department of Social Welfare, College Road, Sligo.

People who Cannot Get Benefit

There is no form of social welfare benefit for deserted husbands, unmarried parents or prisoners' spouses. This seems particularly unfair because, even if you have paid social welfare contributions, you cannot get benefit on the same grounds as if you were unemployed or a deserted wife. As the allowance rate is lower than the benefit rate this ruling discriminates against these categories of people.

Your Right to Appeal Social Welfare Decisions

If you apply for social welfare benefit or assistance and are turned down you can write to the Department of Social Welfare stating that you wish to appeal and enclosing your application. Most appeals are decided on the basis of written applications. If you are called to a hearing, you have the right to be represented and should seek the advice of your social worker, if you have one, or ask for help from your local community information centre. Individual Appeals Officers retain the discretion to decide whether or not appeals are dealt with in writing or by oral hearing. But in practice, if you ask for an oral hearing you will be granted one. If you are not satisfied with the appeals procedure or with how your case is being handled you could take the matter up with the Ombudsman or your local TD, with the former in writing and the latter either by writing or attending his or her clinic. Most TDs hold local constituency clinics, usually on Friday evenings or Saturday mornings. Enquire from your local Party headquarters, or consult local newspapers for details. You must have availed of the social welfare appeals system before the Ombudsman can investigate your case.

The Social Welfare Act, 1990, made provision for the establishment of a separate Social Welfare Appeals Office. The Minister may direct that an oral hearing be given, if he/she considers the case warrants it.

If your Spouse Dies

Contributory Widow's Pension

This is payable regardless of your age if the contribution conditions are satisfied on either your own PRSI or on that of your late husband at the date of his death. The two insurance records may not be combined in order to qualify. The Pension is payable for as long as you remain a widow and do not cohabit. Entitlement is not affected by any other income you may have, either from employment or from any other source. If you become entitled to a retirement or old age pension you can choose to continue receiving your Contributory Widow's Pension instead, if it is to your advantage, but not both. A Contributory Widow's Pension should be claimed within three months of your husband's death, as arrears of pension will not be paid for a longer period. Claim forms are available in Post Offices and should be completed and returned to the Department of Social Welfare, College Road, Sligo.

If you are not entitled to a Contributory Widow's Pension, you may qualify for the Lone Parent's Allowance, provided you satisfy the means test and conditions (see page 16).

If you are in receipt of the Lone Parent's Allowance, you may be eligible to claim for footwear and clothing for your children, reduction in your differential rent if you are in local authority housing, supplementary welfare, butter vouchers, and/or a fuel allowance in winter. Apply to your local health board office. Butter vouchers and the fuel allowance are available from the Department of Social Welfare.

Tax Relief

If, as a widow/widower, you pay tax, or are in taxable employment, you are entitled to claim a Single Parent Family Tax Allowance. Cohabiting will disallow you.

Extra Allowances

Free electricity or gas allowance, free TV licence and telephone rental are available to those aged sixty-six years and over who are receiving a social welfare pension and who are living alone or living with certain people.

Free travel is available to all on reaching sixty-six years of age.

Death Grant

This is a payment, based on your spouse's or your own PRSI contributions, made on the death of an insured person, the husband or wife of an insured person, the widow or widower of an insured person, or a child under eighteen years of an insured person. Send your claim within three months of the death to the Department of Social Welfare, Gandon House, Amiens Street, Dublin 1. You may be able to get assistance with the funeral costs under the Supplementary Welfare Scheme (see page 30).

Child Benefit (Children's Allowance)

This is paid monthly, usually to the mother or the full-time carer. You may continue to receive this Benefit until the child is aged sixteen years or up to eighteen years if the child is in full-time education or is physically or mentally handicapped. It is not means-tested or taxable. Claim forms are available in Post Offices, and Benefit is also paid out from there. Claims should be made within three months after the month the child is born or becomes a member of your family, as arrears will not be paid for longer than this.

Unmarried Families

This book is mainly directed at people without partners —but what happens under social welfare if you are living with someone and you and he/she are not married? You are not entitled to any of the single parent benefits if you are cohabiting. You may, however, be regarded as a dependent of your partner if you are looking after a child/children. Or you may have some entitlements from your marriage.

If you have been receiving the dependent spouse and child portions of your spouse's social welfare benefit, you can continue to receive these.

If you are living with someone to whom you are not married and you have children, the Department of Social Welfare will generally treat you as married. He or she can claim social welfare benefit for you and the children (even if the children are not his/hers), once you are wholly or mainly supported by him/her and you take care of the children.

Be aware that the tax system does not apply the same criteria.

Unemployment Benefit (UB)

In order to qualify for Unemployment Benefit, you must be capable of, available for, and actively seeking work, and have made sufficient pay-related social insurance (PRSI) contributions. You must also be aged under sixty-six years. You cannot qualify on the basis of your spouse's contributions. If you feel that you have been turned down unfairly, you should appeal immediately. Do not tell the employment exchange that you would prefer part-time work; they may then consider that you do not want full-time work and you may not get Benefit.

To apply for UB you need a P45 document which you should have received from your employer on your last day at work. You should also bring your P60, detailing your income to the end of the last tax year. If you qualify, you will receive the payments for a maximum period of fifteen months. Apply immediately, even if you do not have these documents.

You may also be entitled to pay-related benefit. Ask for leaflet SW51 or contact Pay-Related Benefit Section (see Appendix One).

Unemployment Assistance (UA)

You may be eligible for Unemployment Assistance if you are unemployed and do not qualify for or have exhausted your entitlement to Unemployment Benefit. In order to qualify you must be aged between eighteen and sixty-six, be actively seeking work and satisfy a means test. For this means test, maintenance payments are treated as cash income but the house that you live in is not assessed unless you receive some income from letting part of it. If board and lodging is being provided

for you by another person—a parent, a relative or friend
—this may be assessed as part of your income.

To get UA you must first have a Qualification
Certificate which shows your means. Apply for this even
if you are still in work but know that you will soon be
unemployed. Applications for the Certificate and for the
UA payment should be sent to your local Employment
Exchange Office (see phone book).

The Means Test

When you apply for a means-tested social welfare
payment, details of your means are requested on the
relevant forms. The stringency of the means test varies
depending on the payment you are seeking. The
Department of Social Welfare's booklet *Guide to Social
Welfare Services* outlines the means test, what counts
and does not count as means, and the formulas they
apply. The test for Unemployment Assistance is one of
the most difficult to obtain. Once you have applied and
completed your form, you will normally be visited at
home by a social welfare officer. He or she will seek
further details of your means and will ask to see bank
books and receipts of purchases made. It is rather
degrading to feel that your whole personal life is now
open for inspection, but if you need and want that
payment it is in your own interest to co-operate. The
social welfare officer is merely doing a job. If you do not
understand how the subsequent payment amount is
arrived at, ask. If you disagree with their assessment,
you may appeal to the Social Welfare Appeals Office.

The health boards have a separate but broadly
similar means test system. However, each separate

health board has its own rules for applying the means test; these are not co-ordinated and there is no statutory basis for them.

Meanwhile...

While all these forms and details are being processed (and it may take some time), you and your family have got to live. If you have no money, contact your nearest health centre and ask about Supplementary Welfare. The person to see is the community welfare officer.

Supplementary Welfare

If you have insufficient money to meet your needs or those of your dependents you can apply for payment from the Supplementary Welfare Allowance scheme. In order to qualify you will have to:

- apply for any other benefits you may be entitled to, for example, Unemployment Assistance
  and
- register for work with FÁS if you are of working age
  and
- satisfy a means test.

There is a statutory minimum payment, in line with the basic Unemployment Assistance payment, to which you are entitled if you have no means. If you have low means you will be entitled to an allowance to bring your income up to the basic rate allowance. If you have no other income and have claimed a social welfare benefit or pension, but it has not yet been paid, you may qualify for SWA while you are waiting. A single payment may be made in exceptional circumstances to meet an urgent need.

How it is Paid

The community welfare officer attends your local health centre at set times during the week. It is not necessary to have an appointment. You go in, state your case and, generally, you will be told to return the following week (or later that week) when a decision on your eligibility will be given. If considered eligible, you will receive a cheque payment from the officer. In some special circumstances a cash payment can be made. If your financial situation is critical, the community welfare officer can, at his/her discretion, make an immediate payment.

Supplements

If your income is too low to meet special needs such as particular diets or heating, you may get a weekly supplement. Each case is decided on its merits. A letter from your doctor will usually be required as evidence.

Rent Allowance

If you are in rented accommodation and cannot pay the rent, the welfare officer may be able to assist you. You will not be subsidised to live in a luxury apartment, but even modest accommodation is hard to find and expensive, so do ask. There is a separate social welfare rent allowance payable to tenants who are living in a dwelling where the rent was controlled before 1982 and who satisfy certain conditions. Apply to the Rent Allowance Section, Oisín House, 212-213 Pearse Street, Dublin 2.

If you live in local authority housing, the Corporation or Council may be able to help if you ask to have the rent reduced.

Exceptional Needs Payment

If you are faced with a particular expense which is beyond your means, you may apply for this payment. The types of expenses which may be considered are:

- a pram or bedding for a baby
- arrears of rent, electricity or gas
- cost of travel to visit a family member in jail or hospital
- funeral expenses
- expenses resulting from fire or flood damage.

How to Appeal a Supplementary Welfare Decision

If you apply for Supplementary Welfare and are turned down, you can appeal the decision by writing to The Appeals Officer, at your local health board or at 37 Castle Street, Dublin 2. If you are unsure of how to state your case to the appeals officer, the social worker in your area will assist you. The major flaw in this procedure as it operates at present is that your appeal is heard by the health board which initially rejected your application. There is, as yet, no independent appeals tribunal.

Family Income Supplement (FIS)

If you work but are on a low wage and have a family to support you may be eligible for extra money from the FIS scheme. To qualify for this weekly cash payment you have to be working full-time for an employer (i.e. at least twenty hours a week—hours worked by both partners can be combined); you must be receiving Child Benefit for at least one child and your average weekly income must be below the specified amounts. FIS is normally 60 per cent of the difference between your gross weekly family income and the income limit for your family size. Lone parents qualify on the same criteria. However, if you are receiving a Lone Parent's Allowance, this will be included as income. Casual or seasonal employment does not qualify for FIS.

How FIS is Paid

FIS is paid to the worker by an order book similar to a Child Benefit book which can be cashed at a Post Office of your choice.

FIS is paid for fifty-two weeks while you continue working. During that time it is not affected by changes in family circumstances or short periods of illness. At the end of the fifty-two weeks you can reapply for FIS if you are still eligible.

FIS application forms are available in any Post Office and should be completed and sent to: Family Income Supplement Section, Oisín House, 212-213 Pearse Street, Dublin 2.

What Else are you Entitled to?

Fuel Allowance

If you get a Supplementary Welfare Allowance or are dependent on long-term social welfare or health board payments, you may also be entitled to a fuel allowance. The scheme operates from mid October to mid April. Where two or more people who would qualify individually are living in the same household, a single fuel allowance will be paid to that household. Contact the Department of Social Welfare, Áras Mhic Dhiarmada, Dublin 1.

Help with Electricity or Gas Bills

In cases of hardship, the welfare officer can, at his/her discretion, give payments towards arrears outstanding on electricity or gas bills. You must prove that you are making genuine efforts to reduce the bill yourself.

Footwear and Clothing for your Children

This is part of the Supplementary Welfare Allowance scheme, available to school-going children. No one will ask you whether your kids have sound shoes or adequate clothing: you must apply. Enquire at your local health board office, if you feel you would qualify, and be most insistent that they listen to your case. Children's shoes are expensive and children's feet need the protection of good shoes. This scheme operates in the winter, beginning in September or October.

School-Books

A free school-book scheme is administered by your child's school principal at his/her discretion. You should approach the principal at the beginning of the school year and explain your situation so that some or all of your child's books can be supplied free of charge. As an alternative, try to ensure that you obtain at least some of the books second-hand; the class teacher or neighbours' children may be able to help. Many book-shops sell second-hand school-books alongside the new ones, but do get your list in in June or July rather than leaving it until the last week in August when the queues are forming. Ask the community welfare officer or social worker at your local health board office about help towards the cost of school uniforms.

School Milk

Find out if your child's school participates in the subsidised milk scheme which is open to all primary and secondary schools and some pre-school groups.

School Transport

School transport is provided in certain areas of the country based on the numbers of children of eligible age and the distance from the nearest suitable primary or post-primary school. This service is free for children of parents with medical cards; if it is not available they can travel free by public transport. You must send your medical card with your application to C.I.E. Non-medical card families must pay for the service.

Exam Fees

The arrangements for these are somewhat similar to the free school-books scheme. The school principal administers a discretionary alleviation scheme to help pupils in need. In 1990, pupils attending a post-primary school and repeating the Leaving Certificate pay a course fee and an examination fee. If you already have a medical card, your child will be exempt from the course fee and will have to pay only the exam fee (currently £33).

Help Agencies

Society of St Vincent de Paul

There are branches of this organisation in most towns and they can be contacted through their headquarters (see Appendix One) or by enquiring locally. Your local social worker or clergyman can put you in touch, if you prefer. The Society helps those in need, assisting with clothes, shoes, bedding and household equipment. They will also contribute towards the cost of school uniforms or such items as a pram or a cot.

Protestant Aid

This is a charity similar to the above and, despite its name, one which helps people of any denomination. Most people are referred by a social worker, clergy of any denomination or a subscriber to Protestant Aid. They provide financial assistance towards payment of secondary school fees and uniforms and will contribute towards heating costs. (See Appendix One.)

How to Find Out if you are Eligible for Social Welfare

Many people do not claim for benefits to which they are entitled and for which they or their spouse have paid over the years through their insurance contributions (PRSI). One way to find out if you qualify is to apply, or ring or visit the Department of Social Welfare. There are thirty-four social welfare information centres throughout the country, or you can contact the Information Service, Department of Social Welfare, Áras Mhic Dhiarmada, Store Street, Dublin 1 (see Appendix One).

If there is any one thing that is vital to your existence or that of your children, then apply for it. Ask at the health centre or talk to your clergyman or doctor. Social welfare officials rarely inform people of their entitlements so you must ferret them out for yourself. This may take time, patience and perseverance: you will have to learn not to be ashamed or shy to ask. The bureaucratic system behaves like a fortress expecting to be besieged by demands. Yet the irony is that many people are too timid or uninformed to apply for entitlements and often do not question the officials who are supposed to be helping them.

Health

Health Board Services

Medical Cards

If you have not already got one, apply at once for a medical card. These are issued to people who, because of their lack of income, are entitled to the full range of health board services without charge. These services include the family doctor, prescribed drugs and medicines, hospital out-patient services and in-patient services in a public ward, and maternity and infant welfare services. Application should be made to the Medical Card Section of your local health board office.

You will be required to declare your income from all sources. Investments and savings are not counted, but interest received on income from these sources will be. Income limits refer to your total income before tax. The health board will advise you about income levels, various allowances for children, housing expenses and, sometimes, reasonable expenses which you pay out in travelling to work, since these too may be taken into account. You are also entitled to dental, optical and aural services. However, due to cutbacks in staff and facilities in the health services these entitlements are not always as accessible as they should be.

Single people aged sixteen and over, if living with medical card holders, qualify for a medical card in their own right. If the young person has an income, she will be means-tested on that, and may qualify. Get an application form from your local health board office. If turned down for a medical card, you can appeal on medical grounds, by way of a doctor's letter, or if your circumstances change.

Medical Card Means Test Appeals Procedure

At the time of writing (May 1990), the Minister for Health was proposing a new appeals system for the means test for medical cards, due to be implemented before the end of 1990.

If you already get a State allowance such as a Lone Parent's Allowance, or a Disabled Person's Maintenance Allowance, you would generally qualify for a medical card without another means test. However, this varies among health boards. If you think you may be eligible among health boards. If you think you may be eligible but are not sure, apply anyway, and if turned down, ask for a full explanation.

Choosing a Doctor

When entitlement to a medical card is confirmed you will have a choice of doctors in your locality. You will be given instructions about registering with a doctor and getting prescriptions free of charge. Choose a doctor near you; it saves time and money when you need his/her services. If for some reason you wish to change your doctor, inform the health board office of your new choice. If this second doctor accepts you as a patient, the board will handle the details of the transfer, including informing the first that you are no longer his/her patient.

Children in Hospital

The health board may provide travel vouchers for medical card holders whose children are in hospital or institutional care in order to allow them to visit.

Help with Medical Bills if you Don't Qualify

Even if you do not qualify for a medical card, in certain circumstances (for instance where you incur exceptionally heavy medical costs), you can apply to your local health board for help with medical bills.

The £10 Hospital Charge

As an out-patient you must pay £10 on your first visit to

the out-patient department. You then do not have to pay for subsequent visits for the same problem. This is an annual charge.

As an in-patient you have to pay £10 per day for maintenance in a public ward, subject to a maximum of £100 in one year.

Those Who Do Not Have to Pay the £10 Charge

The following are exempt from the charge:

- medical card holders
- children who qualify for free drugs and medicine for their particular long-term illness
- children attending out-patient departments because of defects discovered at school health examinations
- children up to six weeks old
- women receiving maternity services
- people receiving treatment or medicine for infectious diseases.

In cases of hardship the charge may be waived. Apply to your local health board if you think you are eligible.

Private Health Insurance

The Voluntary Health Insurance Board (VHI) is a statutory, non-profit-making body set up to offer health insurance to those people who either are outside the scope of the Health Acts or require private treatment and accommodation.

It is possible that you and your family have been

members. Usually, while the family are all members of the scheme, it is the husband who is the subscriber, which means that he has been responsible for all dealings, correspondence and payments. This can raise problems on the death of your husband or when a couple separate.

In the event of the death of a subscriber, payments for the remainder of the subscription year are waived and the widow is given full cover for the rest of the year free. Should she then wish to join the VHI as a subscriber she is entitled to do so. If the husband was a member of a group scheme, paying through his company or a professional organisation at a 10 per cent concessionary discount rate, then the widow is also entitled to the group rate.

Where a husband deserts or a couple separate it is up to the wife to enquire as to her entitlements. If her husband deletes her name from the policy or ceases making payments, she is no longer covered. In the case of a claim being made, all dealings will be with the subscriber only, so you may be obliged to come to an arrangement with your husband about health cover for yourself and your children. Alternatively, you may wish to become a subscriber in your own right. Queries should be sent to the VHI. (See Appendix One.)

Maintenance

Maintenance is a sum of money paid by one spouse to the other—usually by the husband to the wife. It is a contribution towards the support of (a) the spouse who receives it and (b) any dependent children of the marriage. In some cases maintenance is paid only in respect of the children. In certain situations, a wife is required to pay maintenance to her husband.

How to Get It

If you can show that your spouse has failed to provide such maintenance as is proper in the circumstances, you can take him/her to court. Under the Family Law (Maintenance of Spouses and Children) Act, 1976, both spouses are responsible for the maintenance of their children and each other in proportion to their means. If only one spouse is earning and does not maintain the family, then the other spouse has recourse to law to demand this right. Children are treated in law as dependents until they reach sixteen years of age or longer if they are in full-time education or are handicapped. To qualify, you have to be a spouse; if you have a recognised foreign divorce or a civil annulment you cannot seek maintenance under this Act.

If you cannot afford a solicitor apply for legal aid at your nearest legal aid centre (see Appendix One). Usually a case in the District Court will be heard within six to eight weeks after you have issued the summons. It is possible to represent yourself in court but do seek legal advice first. (See also Chapter Four.) The Circuit Court can award higher maintenance payments (depending on the circumstances of the case) but it usually takes longer to get a hearing. Again, seek legal advice.

When deciding on a Maintenance Order in respect of a spouse and/or any dependent children, the court must take into account the income, earning capacity (if any), property and other financial resources of the spouses, and of any dependent children of either parent as well as the dependent children of the family; they must also consider the financial and other responsibilities of the spouses towards each other and towards any dependent children and their needs, including the need for care and attention. Mostly, the courts are concerned with "need," and will seek to provide for a dependent spouse while at the same time trying to ensure that the paying spouse will have enough money for his/her own support.

You can apply to the court for maintenance under this Act even if you are not separated from your spouse, for example where the earning spouse is drinking or gambling the family income and not providing reasonable maintenance for the family.

If your husband has set up home with another woman and has one or more children of that (or any other) relationship, he has no legal obligation to support the woman, but he does have a legal obligation to support any child of which he is the father and the court will take this into account in determining how much maintenance he should be obliged to pay.

If you are not already legally separated, you may prefer to take a Judicial Separation case which will cover maintenance, custody, property and other issues in one action. (See page 91.)

How Maintenance is Paid

When a court awards you maintenance it will probably be as a sum to be paid periodically, i.e. weekly or monthly. You can then decide whether you want the money sent to you directly or paid through the District

43

Court office.

Getting the money paid through the court means that the spouse paying it sends it to your local District Court office. The court clerk will then send it on to you by cheque. There are several advantages in having your maintenance paid this way. Firstly, if the payments are in arrears the court clerk is aware of the fact and can act promptly by issuing a summons (at your request). Secondly, the court keeps a record of all payments made. If a payment does not arrive or the amount is wrong the court clerk will, at your request, contact your spouse. This is a more businesslike and less confrontational method of handling the situation.

Maintenance and Tax

All maintenance payments are made without the deduction of income tax; but the maintenance received by one spouse for his/her own support is treated as income for tax purposes, whilst maintenance received for children is not taxed in the hand of the custodial parent but is treated as income of the person giving it.

Desertion

Since the Judicial Separation and Family Law Reform Act, 1989 became law, the court can make a Maintenance Order even if the applicant has deserted the other spouse if it is of the opinion that a refusal to make the Order would be unjust. Up until then, the court had no choice but to refuse the Order once desertion was shown.

Constructive Desertion

If your spouse has behaved in such a way as to make life

utterly intolerable for you, i.e. with mental or physical violence, drunkenness or adultery which forces you to leave the family home, then that is constructive desertion on your part. Or if your spouse throws or locks you out of the house, preventing your re-entry (presuming there is no Barring Order against you), then you are in constructive desertion and will still be eligible to apply to the court for maintenance. However, if you fear that your spouse may use the fact of your leaving to try to get your maintenance claim disallowed, you should obtain practical evidence as to the circumstances of your leaving. If there is someone who has witnessed violence or threats of violence towards you, or you have a letter or evidence from a doctor, social worker or the police of your mental and physical state at the time of leaving, it will be of help in a court situation if your eligibility for maintenance is being queried.

Adultery

The Judicial Separation and Family Law Act, 1989 states that in deciding whether to grant maintenance and how much, the court must consider the general conduct of either partner. Adultery committed by the applicant spouse would be a consideration but the court is now more likely to assess the relationship and situation in general rather than rule out maintenance for the applicant spouse in such circumstances, as tended to be the case.

Attachment of Earnings Order

If the payments are made erratically and if, most importantly, your spouse is an employee, you can apply to have an Attachment of Earnings Order made. This means that your maintenance will be deducted from your spouse's salary before he/she receives the pay-packet. An Attachment Order cannot be made at the original hearing; a summons for one can be issued only if the maintenance debtor has failed to comply with the order. The Family Law (Maintenance of Spouses and Children) Act, 1976 provides that the employer of the maintenance debtor must comply with the Attachment Order.

If your spouse is self-employed, regularly changes his/her job, is unemployed or will not work, then it is most important to keep the court clerk informed if you notice that the payments fall behind. The court clerk is a busy individual dealing with possibly dozens of maintenance cheques every week along with all his/her other court duties. So do not wait for him/her to notice that you are receiving no money. A telephone call or visit to the court office is usually sufficient. Arrears of maintenance should be chased up as soon as possible. You can claim only a maximum of six months' arrears in the District Court, so if you leave it too long you may not receive all your money.

If your Spouse is on the Dole

The Department of Social Welfare has made provision for the spouses of unemployed people who are defaulting in their maintenance payments. If your husband is receiving Unemployment Benefit or Assistance and is not forwarding the wife and child portions to you under the Maintenance Order, you can apply to the Department of Social Welfare to have these portions paid directly to you. If you are not sure whether or not he is claiming, ask the Department.

Write to the office where your husband is drawing his unemployment payment, state your case and enclose a copy of the court order for maintenance. The Department will then ensure that you receive the payments due to you.

If your Spouse Lives Abroad

If a defaulting spouse is living in the United Kingdom, the reciprocal Maintenance Orders Act of 1974 allows for a Maintenance order issued by an Irish court to be served through a magistrates' court in any part of the UK. A spouse can proceed to sue for maintenance provided he/she has an address or some means of contacting the other spouse in Great Britain.

Maintenance Orders can be enforced in EC countries under the Jurisdiction of Courts and Enforcements of Judgements (European Committee No. 2 Bill) 1987, which was ratified in 1988. The Family Law District Court office in Dolphin House, East Essex Street, Dublin 2 will fill in the forms and initiate action on your behalf. The service is free. Enforcement proceedings in British courts will also be taken (free of charge) by the District Court.

Changing the Amount you are Paid

An existing Maintenance Order may be changed. If your spouse gets an increase in salary and the maintenance order is several years old and does not have a "cost of living index-linked clause" you can apply to the court for a Variation Order. A spouse whose salary or income has dropped or whose circumstances have changed can also apply for a reduction in the payments, especially if the other spouse begins to earn an appreciable salary. If you wish to apply for a Variation Order the court clerk will be able to inform you of the procedures involved and give you the appropriate forms to complete.

Discharge of a Maintenance Order

The Maintenance Order may be discharged at the request of either party if new circumstances exist or if it appears to the court that, having regard to the record of payments and other circumstances, the person or persons receiving the payments will not be adversely affected if the payments cease. The Order could also be discharged if the recipient spouse deserted or could possibly be discharged if the recipient committed adultery.

Lump Sum Settlement

If your spouse wants to pay you a lump sum in settlement as maintenance, do nothing before consulting a lawyer. A lump sum may not take into account inflation, unforeseen crises such as accidents, illness or a sudden change in the financial circumstances of the payer or the recipient. A lump sum or one-off payment does not preclude either spouse suing for maintenance even if there is an agreement between them stating that they have abandoned this right. See also "Judicial Separation," page 91.

The Effects of Desertion and Adultery on Maintenance

Desertion or adultery by a spouse do not affect the other spouse's liability to contribute towards the maintenance of any of his dependent children in the former's custody. If the wife refused maintenance has custody of dependent children then her husband may have to support her indirectly through the maintenance paid to her for the support of the children.

Maintenance if you are a Single Mother

Since the introduction of the Status of Children Act, 1987, all mothers—married or unmarried—may now seek maintenance under the Family Law (Maintenance of Spouses and Children) Act, 1976 in respect of the children.

For unmarried mothers the following regulations apply:

Evidence given by the mother: The court may make a Maintenance Order if it is satisfied on the balance of probabilities that the man is the father. If there is evidence corroborating the mother's then she is more likely to succeed, but the lack of such evidence is no longer an absolute bar to success.

Abolition of time limits: Under earlier legislation a claim for maintenance had to be made within three years of the birth of the child. Now, either parent may sue for maintenance any time until the child reaches sixteen years or twenty-one years if in full-time education. There is no age limit if the child is physically or mentally handicapped.

Mothers who unsuccessfully sought maintenance under the old Affiliation Orders Act may be able to apply under the new Act. Seek legal advice.

Lump Sum Settlement

As with married parents, either unmarried parent has the right to sue for maintenance of the child even if they have already agreed to the payment and acceptance of a lump sum (see page 48.)

A parent, married or unmarried, may apply to the court for a lump sum payment of up to £750 for birth or death expenses of a dependent child.

Maintenance Agreements

Under the Family Law (Maintenance of Spouses and Children) Act, 1976, the parents of a dependent child who are not married to each other can enter into an agreement for one parent to make periodical payments towards the maintenance of the child. This agreement can be made a rule of court and become a legally binding Maintenance Order.

The same rules attaching to a Maintenance Order then apply, i.e. it is possible to apply to the court for a Variation Order, an Interim Order or an Attachment of Earnings Order (see page 45).

Work

If you get maintenance, social welfare payments or a pension, but it is still not enough to live on, then finding another source of income will be a priority.

If you Work Already

You may already have a job. If so, how much will it be

affected by your changed circumstances? It may be difficult to keep to an exact schedule, work overtime, attend impromptu meetings or travel out of town or abroad. It is advisable to inform your employer of your family situation at an early stage. You can explain your needs, such as a more flexible timetable and plenty of advance notice of meetings or business trips. Assure your employer that the work will be done; it is just your routine you wish to alter, not your workload.

What Kind of Work?

What you do will depend on your circumstances. If you have worked before marriage or have a profession or training in some area, then perhaps you could pick up where you left off.

If not, investigate night study courses, correspondence courses and in particular the Government-sponsored re-training schemes. FÁS, the Training and Employment Authority, runs special courses for women who have been out of the work-force for some time, may need retraining or have not necessarily decided what kind of work they would like to do. These courses are designed to help women reach important decisions about work.

Can you work full-time or part-time and for how many or which hours per day or per week? With part-time work check your eligibility for pay-related social insurance. If you work less than eighteen hours per week, you may not be eligible for some or any social welfare benefits due to lack of contributions.

How far can you afford to travel to work considering travelling costs in time as well as money? What type of work can you do, bearing in mind that you have a family to care for and a home to run as well? If you are too exhausted to face the dinner, the children's homework, or even the children themselves, then a rethink of priorities and a change of job is called for.

If going out to work is a must, and you have children, then there are other important aspects to be considered. One is child-care and whether this needs to be full-time or part-time, say after school hours only. You cannot put seven and ten-year-olds in a crèche but they do still need minding. Even the best minders need holidays or get sick, delayed, bored with the job. So can you line up back-up care in emergencies? Some people make arrangements with relations or friends. The question of child-care is considered in more detail later. (See "Child-minding," page 140.)

Another aspect is just how far you are prepared to put up with poor working conditions, hours or pay, in order to hold down a job. Many unscrupulous employers exploit women who are desperate to work and, if you agree to work less than a full week, make sure that you are happy with the arrangement. As a part-timer you may not be protected by employment regulations in the same way as full-time workers.

Finally, you will probably have to consider your children's feelings about your going out to work. It is very important to know that they are happy with their minder. If they are unhappy find out why. If they fret, the chances are that you will not be able to concentrate on your job and your work will suffer. If possible discuss the situation with them and find a minder you both like.

Working at Home

There are many jobs which women do in their own homes which enable them to combine child-care with making a living. These include cooking, sewing, child-minding, typing, running a playgroup, hairdressing, taking in lodgers, bed and breakfast, translating, computer work and tuition. If you have a particular skill which you think you can sell, sit down and work out on paper what it will cost in terms of time, space, purchase or hire of equipment or even staff. How much can you charge, what are the overheads and expenses? How much will you have left after paying tax and PRSI? Bear in mind that if you use your home for business purposes you may have to apply for "change of use" planning permission; you may be liable for local authority rating; and you must ensure that your household insurance policy covers your business activities.

Looking for a Job

Register with FÁS Employment Services Offices (see phone book for local office address) and with an employment agency in your area, if there is one, or in the nearest town. However, if transport to or from work is a problem, or if you must work around your children's schedule, specify this when you sign on.

Newspapers are an obvious source of job advertisements, so scour them—all of them, every day, in the library if you cannot afford to buy them—and act promptly if you see anything likely. Supermarkets have notice-boards, so study them regularly and place an advertisement there offering your services. Some newspapers also have a "job-seeker" column, so place your advert there too. Let people know that you are looking for work and what your skills are. Many jobs are not advertised at all. Type (or get typed) a neatly laid out **curriculum vitae**; get several photocopies made and enclose one with each handwritten letter of application you send. On the depressing assumption that this will be the last you hear about that particular job, because most advertisers do not even acknowledge receipt of applications, keep looking, keep applying and keep cool. Do not take it as a personal rejection or an estimation of your lack of ability and worth if you hear nothing or get turned down. Unfortunately, many employers will hesitate to employ anyone who is not already working. They need not necessarily be working at their chosen profession or at the level of their capabilities, but the fact that they are working implies a degree of effort and commitment that most employers will recognise.

Managing Your Money

Income Tax

Almost everyone who works has to pay income tax. Unless you are self-employed your tax will be deducted at source. This system is known as PAYE (Pay As You Earn). Tax-free allowances are given for various reasons: for instance, if you are paying off a mortgage, have insurance policies or voluntary health cover, or incur particular expenses as a result of the work that you do which are not met by your employer. There is a special one-parent family allowance available to any lone parent, male or female. There are also allowances for incapacitated children, dependent aged relatives and some relief for the children of low-income taxpayers. If you pay tax through the PAYE system, the Revenue Commissioners will send you an income tax form each year to complete. You can ask for a new form if you have a new claim during the year. From the information you supply they will calculate how much tax your employer should deduct from your salary before he/she pays you each week or month. You will be sent a **Certificate of Tax Free Allowances** so that you can check for yourself that everything you are entitled to is included before you pass it on to your employer. When you begin work you will have to call or write to the appropriate tax office (ask your employer) giving details of your earnings, so that a certificate can be issued; otherwise your employer will have no information about your allowances and he/she may have to deduct tax from your earnings at the emergency rate. If you are self-employed you are expected to declare your income by self-assessment each year. Ask the Revenue Commissioners for the appropriate forms. These should be submitted each year on 1 October.

A Taxing Problem

If the whole business of tax defeats you, Financial Information Service Centres (FISC) assist in family finance matters the way FLAC has helped in family law. The service is run by young accountants who operate about a dozen centres around the country. The service, which is free and completely confidential, provides advice on tax and family budgeting. Contact FISC for details of your nearest centre (see address in Appendix One).

Do try to manage your own money instead of simply saying "I'm hopeless with money" and abdicating responsibility for your personal finances. Make it your business to find out what you need to know, ask the bank manager to help you plan a budget or talk to FISC. If you do hand the financial reins to someone else and they drink, gamble, speculate or unwisely invest it, what come-back do you have? If you are afraid that you might drink, gamble, speculate or unwisely invest it yourself then seek financial help immediately.

Planning—How to find what you want, when you need it

Every person should have a filing system. This need not be an elaborate system but it must be a tidy one. A shoe-box is better than nothing. Keep a record of all letters written to and received from official bodies, with dates and references clearly marked; also receipts of payments and letters of advice on insurance, hire purchase, TV licence, car or life insurance and the like. Keep a legal file with a record of all correspondence, dates and details of any important telephone calls and receipts of monies paid. A medical file should contain hospital and clinic attendance cards, vaccination records and so on. Keep another for your children's school reports and one for your CV and job applications.

It is both reassuring and time-saving to have these details to hand when needed. Keep a diary (preferably a page a week one) and record all dental, medical, job and legal appointments. Also note the dates and amounts of regular bills due (oil, rent, electricity or gas) and mark off the amount and date when paid. Your life is going to be too busy to remember everything, so write it down. It also means you can budget for the coming year on the basis of the figures to hand for the current year. It may sound boring and fussy, but it is important. If, for example, you become embroiled in a court case or are applying for Supplementary Welfare or a medical card, these facts and figures will come in very useful.

3

A Roof Over Your Head

For some lone parents the biggest problem is housing;
how to get and keep a roof over your head now that you
are responsible for ensuring that you and the children
have somewhere to live. You may want to stay on in the
family home, or you may prefer to pull out altogether,
starting again somewhere else; indeed you may have no
choice. Whatever you decide, the following are some
facts on accommodation you will need to know.

The Family Home

In the eyes of the law "the family home" has a precise
meaning. It can be a house that you and/or your spouse
own, but it also includes a house that is leased or
rented, a flat, caravan or mobile home. A residential
public house or shop, a family farmhouse or, indeed, any
dwelling house in which a married couple ordinarily
lives comes under the heading of a "family home." The
Family Home Protection Act, 1976 seeks to ensure that
a spouse and children shall not be unjustly deprived of
the family home in a broken or troubled marriage by the
actions of the other partner.

Rights to the Family Home

The family home under the above Act is broadly defined as the dwelling in which a married couple ordinarily resides. If one spouse leaves the home it continues to be the family home for the purposes of the Act. The term also applies to a dwelling in which a spouse whose protection is at issue ordinarily resides, although it may not be the original family home in which the couple resided.

Ownership of the family home depends on two things:
(1) whose name the property is registered in and
(2) who paid for the property.

A wife who has contributed financially, either directly or indirectly, to the purchase of the property has a beneficial interest in it in proportion to her contribution, even if the home is registered in her husband's name. However, if the property is in the wife's name the husband does not have a beneficial interest, regardless of financial contribution on his part, because there is a presumption of advancement from husband to wife (i.e. that he gave it to her as a gift). This presumption can be rebutted but it is hard to do so and depends on the intention of the spouses at the time the property was put into the wife's name. When the home is registered in both spouses' names they are joint owners.

A husband or wife cannot sell or mortgage the family home without the written consent of the other spouse, no matter whose name the property is registered in and regardless of their respective financial interests in it. However, the spouse's consent can be dispensed with by the court if the court is satisfied that it is being withheld unreasonably; for example, if the other spouse is willing to provide suitable alternative accommodation for the family. The alternative accommodation should be at the same standard as the previous family home if the spouse can afford it and to the highest standard he/she can afford if circumstances have altered. In judging such cases under this Act, the court would take into account factors such as the availability of schools etc., as well as other aspects which the court might consider relevant.

When a family home is being sold or mortgaged, enquiries must be made as to whether the owner has a spouse whose prior consent must be acquired before the transaction can be completed. A spouse can apply to the Registry of Deeds or the Land Registry to have a notice lodged stating that the owner of the property is married and naming the spouse. Solicitors acting for the purchaser of the property would find the notice when carrying out searches and insist on the necessary written consent. One spouse cannot act without the consent of the other in disposing of the property. The court can dispense with the consent in these cases if it is judged to be withheld unreasonably.

Where a family home which is jointly owned is sold, the husband and wife are entitled to equal shares of any profit on the sale. Where the house is in sole ownership, the non-owning spouse will be entitled to a share equal to his/her financial contribution towards its purchase. In cases of dispute legal advice should be sought.

In the case of joint ownership, on the death of one spouse the home becomes the sole property of the other spouse and does not form part of the estate of the deceased.

It is possible to have the family home changed from single to joint ownership (and vice versa); fees are now controlled by the Family Home Protection Act. No stamp duty or registration fee is payable on these transactions; the only cost will be legal fees.

If the house is in joint ownership, both owners are equally responsible for meeting the costs of mortgage repayments, so each spouse is usually made jointly and separately liable for the mortgage repayments under the terms of the mortgage deed.

Where the family home is part of a farm, it and the land or garden on which it stands are protected by the Act and cannot be sold without the consent of both spouses. The farmland is not subject to the Act and landowners may dispose of their land as they please. Where the land is jointly owned other arrangements must be made.

With regard to houses owned by local authorities, most tenancies are granted jointly these days. Where the tenancy is in one name only, it is possible for the local authority to have it changed to joint names if they have a court order.

What happens when the spouse in whose name the house is registered deserts and the other spouse takes over the mortgage repayments? The latter can apply to the court for an order transferring the ownership to his or her own name. The home can still not be sold without the consent of both spouses, unless the court dispenses with the consent of the deserting spouse. When payments fall into arrears the mortgagee (usually the building society or the bank) may ask the court to make an order for the sale of the premises. If the spouse who is not the registered owner is able to pay the arrears and continue the repayments the mortgagee will not be granted the order for sale. The court may order the original owner to transfer interest in the family home to the sole name of the other spouse. However, if neither spouse can discharge the arrears and continue the repayments, the mortgagee will be granted an order for sale of the property.

One gap in the cover provided by the Family Home Protection Act is where one spouse runs up debts and is sued. The creditors may succeed in an application to sell the house in order to claim the amount due to them; but they can only claim an interest in the debtor's half. If you fear that your spouse is running up debts which may jeopardise the family home, consult a solicitor immediately.

The cost of legal action regarding the family home depends on the value of the property and the nature of the proceedings. Depending on your disposable income per week (what you have left after you have fulfilled your normal commitments—rent, rates, mortgage, etc.) you may be eligible for Civil Legal Aid. A wife taking a family home case is not judged on her husband's income. You may still have to pay a certain amount, depending on your circumstances: this will be explained at the Legal Aid Centre.

A Word of Warning

Family home protection legislation refers to a dwelling occupied by one or both members of a **married** couple. It does not cover the home(s) of couples who are **not** married. For unmarried couples buying a house, see page 203.

Where Else Can you Go?

What are the alternatives if you must, for whatever reason, leave the family home?

Back to Mother

For some this is the obvious and ideal solution. For others it is either impossible or unthinkable. If you have very little money and small children and your parents have room and are willing to have you, it could be a heaven-sent opportunity to sort yourself out and find your feet. But it should be seen as at most a temporary arrangement until you can establish a home of your own. Be conscious of the pitfalls as well as appreciative of the advantages. Remember that your parent or parents are getting on in years and have already reared a family; they may have other interests of their own or have become set in their ways. They might treat you like a child and spoil your children. They may go on at length extolling the virtues or enumerating the vices of the absent spouse. They may frown on your attempts to seek a social life or disapprove of your methods of child-rearing. On the other hand they may be of fantastic support and help to you. Either way, you should think carefully before you decide to make a long-term arrangement of your return to the parental nest.

Subsidised Flatlets

There are some subsidised flatlets for single mothers provided by voluntary organisations such as Cherish (see Appendix One for addresses). The flatlets are designed as self-contained, short-stay accommodation but often, because of lack of alternative permanent accommodation, families have no option but to remain in them until they are rehoused by the corporation or county council. Most are reserved for single mothers but other one-parent families may qualify.

A Live-In Job

With a live-in job you solve two problems at one stroke: a job and a place to live. The advantages are obvious. You pay no rent; some or all of your meals may be supplied; there are no transport or travelling problems to get to work. It also means that you have company and are not alone at night, and there may be baby-sitting facilities when you are off duty.

Live-in jobs occasionally suit single parents with one child, and separated or widowed people with or without a child. They are rarely suitable for people with more than two children.

For women without children, there is a fairly broad range of live-in jobs: hotels, hospitals, pubs, nursing homes, as well as "au pair"-type jobs either here or abroad. For those with one or two children the job is likely to be as a home-help or housekeeper in a private home, a residential home or a school. These jobs are advertised in the newspapers but do vet them carefully before you say yes. Ask lots of questions about hours on duty, time off, if and when you can use the cooking/washing facilities, whether you can have visitors, what the extras are, who pays for what, if they will pay your PRSI.

The disadvantages are less obvious. If, for some reason, you do not like the job or the people, you will be faced with the dilemma of giving up both the job and your home. While the idea of company may appear attractive, is there somewhere you can be on your own, especially if you have a child? What happens if you are sick or off duty? Are "time off" and "your room" clearly defined? Can you cook a meal, have friends in, have the radio on at night?

It might be a good idea to have a written agreement between your employer and yourself outlining terms of employment, hours and pay, and including a clause giving you both a trial period of, perhaps, three months or so to see how the arrangement works. This need not be a formal or legally binding agreement, but it should be a written one to which one or both of you can refer if the need arises.

If you are basically an independent sort of person, the confines and restrictions of a live-in job may soon begin to tell on you. It is difficult to feel that you are not at work while you are still on the premises. This is especially true if you work where there are children and have children yourself. You may also find that having your child/children at work with you is a strain, both on them and on you.

I worked for seven months in a children's home when my own children were aged three and four years old. They resented my caring for the other children (all very young); and caring for a large group of children from 8.00 a.m. to 5.30 p.m. each day left me with little time or energy for my own two, who needed all the love and attention I could give them.

Renting from a Private Landlord

Flats and houses in the private sector are expensive and landlords, of flats especially, are not generally noted for their love of "unaccompanied" women and children. Even with a man, children are bad news to most landlords.

If you want rented accommodation, read the evening newspapers (preferably the minute they become available), try local estate agents, ask colleagues or put an advertisement in a local newspaper or on the notice-board of your local supermarket.

When you find a place, you may be asked to pay a deposit—usually one month's rent in advance. The length of the lease, and how much rent you pay and when, is arranged with the landlord or his/her agent. If you pay in cash get a receipt and ask for a rent-book. You may be asked to sign an inventory of contents of the house/flat on arrival. It is also useful to make a list of what you own, especially any furniture, adding from time to time any newly acquired possessions. It is advisable to insure your contents in the flat, as they probably will not be covered in the house insurance.

If your income is insufficient to meet the rent (or mortgage repayments) fully, you may be entitled to Supplementary Welfare (see "Supplementary Welfare" on page 30). They will not subsidise you to live in a luxury apartment but, if the difference between what you can pay and what you are being asked to pay is small, then apply immediately to the local community welfare officer and avoid arrears piling up. If you have any disputes with landlords or problems with tenancy seek advice from Threshold or the Coolock Community Law Centre. (See Appendix One for addresses.)

Renting from the Local Authority

Apply to the corporation or your local county council to be assessed for eligibility for a local authority house or flat. Depending on your location or choice of area, you will probably have to go on a waiting-list; an exception is made for cases of extreme hardship or "special circumstances" (at the local authority's discretion).

Homelessness

You will be considered homeless by the corporation or county council if you have been evicted on foot of a court order, or if you can provide other written proof which will be accepted by the housing authority.

While the local authority may provide housing for a homeless person, it is not under any legal obligation to do so. You may be allocated temporary accommodation and you must accept where they place you. In 1990, 69 per cent of homeless people applying to Dublin Corporation were women on their own with children.

Being housed or rehoused involves a visit by a health inspector to your present abode. A points system operates whereby domestic arrangements are rated; for example, has accommodation got a flush toilet and, if so, how many share it? Sleeping-space and overcrowding are also rated. There are one- , two- and three-bedroom houses and flats. One-bedroom accommodation is usually for older folk, with two- and three-bedroom houses and flats allocated to couples or single parents with one or more children. Couples do not have to be married to apply as a family.

When the local authority is making its periodic assessment of housing needs, it must notify the local health board, so make your needs known to at least one if not both of these bodies. Cities usually have longer waiting-lists for housing than rural areas so, if you would qualify for a house in your own area, consider carefully before you make a mad dash to the city. Some local authorities do not keep a waiting-list but advertise in the local press as new housing schemes are developed.

Evictions

You cannot be evicted from a local authority house or flat without a court order. If, however, you are evicted by the courts then you become the responsibility of the local authority who must arrange for you to be re-housed.

House Purchase Loan Scheme

The primary aim of the loan scheme is to enable people with low incomes to become owners of houses of a "modest standard." This scheme will apply to those who are unable to obtain loans from commercial agencies such as banks, building societies and insurance companies.

It is necessary to produce documentary evidence that a loan has been refused by both a building society and a bank before your application can be considered by the council. The present scheme has three different repayment options with the loan amounts ranging from £21,000 to £27,000. In order to qualify, the applicant's income in the previous year must not have exceeded £10,000. Apply to your local county council.

Housing Grants

If you do not qualify for the above scheme you may, as a first-time purchaser/occupier of a newly built, previously unoccupied house, qualify for the £2,000 housing grant. Apply to Housing Grants, O'Connell Bridge House, Dublin 2.

Hostels/Refuges

There are several women's refuges around the country, the best-known being the Women's Aid (or Family Aid) refuge in Dublin (see Appendix One). These refuges take in women and their children who have had to flee the family home because of violence or threatened violence and abuse. The refuges usually provide short-term accommodation, although a number of them provide "half-way houses" which assist women in re-starting their lives away from their husbands. They are aimed at emergency cases, with families often arriving by taxi or police car in the middle of the night after a domestic battle. The refuges are under-funded and overcrowded but provide a vital safety net to battered wives and terrified children. If you are desperate and urgently need a place to stay, ask the police, the casualty department of your local hospital, or a social worker for the address of your nearest refuge. These are very much emergency forms of accommodation and must be viewed only as stepping-stones to being re-housed.

Some of these refuges carry the status of homelessness, the qualification necessary for re-housing by the corporation or local authority. Thus, any person living in these refuges for three months or more may be considered by the corporation to have maximum points for rehousing, subject to availability. For further information contact Focus Point, a voluntary organisation which works with homeless people (see Appendix One).

Bed-Sitters

If you have children, bed-sitters should be viewed as either temporary or a last resort. They may be ideal, even vital as a short-term roof over your heads, but the lack of space and privacy will depress you and fray your nerves. If you have a baby you will have a lot of washing, with the problem of drying and airing clothes. There will be no escape for you or your children from each other and the strain of living in one room may ruin your health. You may also have to share cooking and bathroom facilities with other tenants. In money terms, a bed-sit may not actually be much cheaper than a flat for what you get.

House-Sharing

House-sharing can be a way of getting the kind of home you want, without taking on all the problems of running a house single-handed.

The most obvious person to share a home with is someone in a similar situation. You could jointly buy a property or share the rent. Obviously, it is important to choose the right type of person to share with: someone with similar attitudes, temperament, tastes and life-style. Groups such as Gingerbread or Cherish may be sources of possible "mates." Do bear in mind that sharing will probably mean sharing everything—food, space, kids, illnesses and such like—so choosing carefully and having a trial period with an "out-clause" is vital before you plunge in. I know one woman who, on separating, immediately advertised for someone to share her house, then discovered that she had no privacy, nothing in common with the sharer, and felt that her home was not her own anymore. I know of others who managed to run a fairly effective co-op-type system; where one mother had the house and let portions of it to two other mothers. Two worked outside the home and the third worked inside, also taking care of the children; each contributed to expenses and overheads. That worked fine until one of the women became pregnant by the husband of one of the others. Communal living can offer tremendous support and solidarity to its participants—or it can be living hell. Several adults under one roof can often be the recipe for disaster, unless they are kindred spirits.

You might consider sharing a house or flat with a man, without there being any intimate relationship. A widower with children or a separated father could well be faced with the problem of whether or not he can keep on his job, meet high rent or mortgage repayments **and** pay a housekeeper. Sharing, while meaning a compromise and a lot of give and take on both sides, puts you on an equal footing. You are not an employee but a partner. Also, the children could benefit from having two "parents," and you and they are relieved of the strain of trying to cope with all the practical problems of single-handed living.

If you share a house with a man, you run the risk of the social welfare authorities (or your husband, if you are separated) viewing it as cohabiting and your welfare payments or maintenance being stopped unless you can prove that you are indeed sharing only the house and not the bed.

Finally, a word of warning. Do not share, combine or otherwise merge your finances with those of your partner/s in any new living arrangement. You should certainly contribute your fair share to the agreed overheads and living expenses, but do it with your own money in your sole control and do not be convinced by any argument to open joint accounts or pool financial resources. Keep your money separate in your name at all times.

Moving House

Moving about from place to place is a traumatic, unsettling and alienating experience. Children need security and continuity in their lives. Uprooting and change can be very distressing, even for many adults, particularly those not so young anymore. That said, it is a known fact that many, if not most, one-parent families move at least once and sometimes many times in search of a home.

The National Association of Widows advises women coming to them not to sell the family home and move, even if memories do hurt. They have found that when order and rationality are restored, home is the vital core and neighbourhood familiarity provides consolation and continuity. The same good advice might apply to someone whose marriage has ended in separation. So if you have a home do consider very carefully before you decide to change it.

Where you choose to live will be dictated by the kind of life-style you want, where you can find employment, the proximity of schools and, of course, what you can afford. Country living may sound rustic, romantic and restful but if you must travel miles to work, schools or shops, how much is it going to cost in time and money? Is there adequate public transport? Are there retraining facilities or night classes if you need them? As against that, rents will be cheaper in small towns or in the country than in cities. Also, in a country area, the option to buy out some small place may more readily present itself and at a lower price.

The important considerations—apart from the house/flat/bed—sit itself—are jobs, buses and trains, schools, shops, libraries, baby-sitters, social amenities, family, friends and relatives. If you already have some of these resources where you are now, think carefully about shifting at all. Moving to a new area means more than just a different house; it means different neighbours, doctor, dentist, milkman—everything. In short, it can be a total change to your way of life. If your child has lost a parent must she suffer the loss of home with all its familiarities as well?

When Moving is a Must

Make a list of everything you own and, if possible, enlist the help of friends. Ask one of them to have your small children and/or pets for the day. If funds are low and you have to pack up yourself, or you must get out in a hurry, large cardboard cartons from the supermarket, reinforced with tape or twine, will cope with most of the household ware. Label each box with the contents. Pack in order of priority use since there will be some items which will not be needed for several days or weeks, while you will want to put your hands on others immediately. Clear labelling is vital.

There are advantages to doing all the packing yourself. If you pack things, you know where to find them later. Thus the alarm clock and the children's school-bags can be located without panic. So, nominate

72

yourself director of operations and assign jobs to your helpers. Do not pack the kettle, the tea-bags and the mugs, you will need them!

Moving house creates a terrible feeling of upset and anti-climax, especially when it comes on the heels of a shattered relationship. So, if possible, arrange for a friend to come and visit for the evening or so following moving in.

Householder Insurance

Even if you think you own nothing of any consequence or value, you should give some thought to insuring your home or, if you live in rented accommodation, its contents. If you are doubtful, just consider what it would cost you to replace, at today's prices, all your accumulated possessions, if the whole lot went up in smoke.

How to Evaluate your Possessions

First sit down and list **everything** you own: furniture, pots and pans, radio, books, jewellery, clothes, children's toys and so on. These should be valued at what they would cost to buy today or (more realistically) at next year's prices. Any auctioneer will value a house, land or furniture for you, a jeweller will value jewellery, both for a fee.

When you know what you want insured and what the value is, approach an insurance broker or company and request the relevant type of insurance. Different insurance companies offer different types of cover at different rates, so shop around for the one best suited to your particular needs. Some companies offer an "index-linked" householder's policy which also gives replacement value (the cost of buying the articles new today) instead of market value (the value of the article less depreciation, wear and tear, etc.). Because the policy is index-linked, the sums assured and your premium will increase in line. An index-linked policy is more expensive but provides more comprehensive cover. The Irish Insurance Association runs a free Insurance Information Service (see Appendix One).

It is wise to notify your insurance company of any substantial purchase or gift—some companies ask you to list items over a stipulated value—or of a significant increase in the value of your house as soon as this occurs; otherwise you may find yourself under-insured.

Mortgage Protection Policy

If you have obtained a mortgage to purchase your home, you can also take out a mortgage protection policy; indeed, this will probably be a condition of your loan. An insurance broker or the building society or bank will advise. Life insurance will be dealt with separately. (See Chapter Nine.)

4

Approaching the Law

Going to a Solicitor

The first solicitor I approached when I separated looked
to be on the senior side of eighty, and received me in
cold, dark Dickensian apartments, the floor littered
with dusty files and legal tomes. His words chill my
blood to this day. Peering at me over rimless spectacles
across the large desk he said, "Go home and your
children will be a consolation to you in your old age." I
was twenty-two years old at the time.

I went to another solicitor who was sympathetic,
patient, kind and charged me very little. But it would
have saved us both time and money if he had said at the
outset that he did not handle family law cases, or even
that he did not wish to handle **my** case. After eighteen
months of going nowhere, I eventually took my case to
the original Free Legal Advice Centre (FLAC) and
subsequently got an order for maintenance in the
District Court.

Later I went to a solicitor who kept my file for a year
and then disappeared, leaving my case and several
others behind in various unfinished stages.

Not all solicitors are so unhelpful or unappreciative of the terrible pressures—practical, emotional and financial—that bedevil separating parents at this time. However, the exceptions appear to be in short supply and great demand. Much of the onus will be on you to keep your case to the fore of your solicitor's mind and on his/her desk.

If you have difficulty in finding a helpful solicitor versed in family law, contact AIM Group for Family Law Reform, who advise people with marital problems and also act as a referral agency to solicitors listed with them who are willing to handle family cases. (See Appendix One for address.)

Be warned though, solicitors can be expensive, so talk money with them **before** discussing the details of your case.

Getting Legal Aid

The State Scheme

A scheme of civil legal aid and advice was set up by the Minister for Justice in 1979, and the first centre opened in Dublin in August 1980. The centres are administered by the Legal Aid Board, and their purpose is to enable people to obtain legal services whatever their income (or lack of it). In other words if you cannot afford to pay a solicitor or the full amount of legal fees then you may qualify for subsidised legal services.

The services which the Civil Legal Aid Board provide include:

■ family law problems—maintenance, custody, judicial separation, violence, etc.

- landlord and tenant problems
- complaints about goods purchased
- problems about a hire purchase agreement
- complaints about the services of a contractor
- making or contesting a will.

How do you Qualify and How Much does it Cost?

The service provided by the Legal Aid Board is not free. If you qualify you will have to make contributions based on your income and your ability to pay. If you are on social welfare, advice will cost you £1, and attending court £15. These contributions are normally payable in advance, except in certain exceptional circumstances when, at the Board's discretion, it may be possible to pay by instalments. Applicants must submit to a means test which specifies strict income limits.

One condition which directly affects many single parents is the fact that "income" includes the "value of other benefits or privileges including the value of free or partly free board." In other words, if a relative or friend offers you accommodation, however temporary or unsuitable, it could affect your eligibility for legal services and therefore your chances of getting access to the courts for maintenance, custody or whatever.

Other Restrictions

As a rule, there is no free choice of solicitor under the scheme, and you must apply to your nearest legal aid centre (see Appendix One). In addition to the twelve main full-time centres, there are several part-time centres around the country, so contact the nearest full-time centre for these addresses and opening hours.

If, for whatever reason, you do not wish to avail of the services of the centre nearest to you, but choose a lawyer at a different centre, any extra expense incurred by you or by the Legal Aid Board will mean an increase in the contribution payable by you for legal services, unless the Board is satisfied that your decision was reasonable.

As a precondition to being granted legal services, you must also sign an agreement to the effect that any damages, money or property recovered as a result of proceedings, or a settlement out of court, will be paid to the Legal Aid Board unless, in the opinion of the Board, it would create severe hardship for the applicant to do so. Property/money not covered by this agreement includes:

- the house where you normally live and your household goods;
- periodical maintenance payments;
- the first £2,500 arrears of maintenance;
- the first £2,500 arrears under the Social Welfare, Health, or Redundancy Acts.

Disputes involving property are excluded from the State legal aid scheme; this could in some cases involve disputes over the family home, in which case you would need a lawyer.

There is a requirement in the scheme that a solicitor working on your behalf must inform the person against whom you are taking the case that an application for legal aid has been made, giving them fourteen days to reply, stating reasons why legal aid should or should not be given. When legal aid is granted, the solicitor must again inform the other party of that fact. In practical terms this means that if you apply for legal aid to take a case for maintenance, custody or whatever against your husband, your solicitor will write to your husband or his solicitor informing him of the fact and giving him fourteen days to come up with a reason why you should or should not be eligible. In such a case it would be possible for your husband, for whatever reason, to stall the entire proceedings by proffering reasons, all of which must be checked by the Legal Aid Board, in an effort to have you declared ineligible. However, the Board has left it to the discretion of the lawyers in the centres whether to give notice to the other party in family cases where it is vital to protect the client's privacy and welfare.

If both spouses want and qualify for legal aid they must attend the same centre, with the possibility of their being allocated the same solicitor. A request for separate solicitors is usually granted even if it means that a solicitor from another centre attends. The alternative is for one of you to travel on to the next centre. If there is a demand for legal aid in an area without a centre, the Legal Aid Board has made provisions for a solicitor to travel there on certain days to see clients by appointment.

How the Scheme Works in Practice

If you want to know more about the scheme, apply to the nearest law centre or the Legal Aid Board (see Appendix One for addresses) for the information sheet which outlines the services, types of cases covered, eligibility regulations, contributions payable and other details. If you want legal aid ask for **form no. 1**, entitled Application for Legal Advice. This is a four-page document seeking details of your income, means, expenditure and suchlike. It can be sent to you by post on request. Having watched several women trying to understand and complete these forms in the reception area of one centre with people coming and going, telephones ringing and so on, I would advise you to have the form sent to you, allowing you to complete it in peace and privacy. In any event, you have also to supply relevant receipts as proof of income and expenditure and these you would not normally carry around with you.

One aspect of the scheme which causes concern to observers and applicants is the way in which contributions by clients are assessed. If, for example, when they assess your means, your contribution is put at the maximum but you have a Maintenance Order which is, in fact, in arrears, do inform the solicitor of this. If what your income should be and what it actually is are two separate things, let the Board know and they will use their discretion to adjust your contribution accordingly.

The Legal Aid Board is ready and willing to use its discretionary powers, particularly in relation to marital cases, and is as flexible as possible in its operation, especially in family cases. Those operating the scheme are coping with a huge deluge of family law cases, many of them complex and muddled in a legal as well as an emotional sense. The scheme is badly under-funded by government and therefore understaffed, and several of the part-time centres have had to close. Even the full-time centres close their doors from time to time to catch up on the backlog of cases.

Nonetheless, this is a service, provided by Government, to help you. There is some red tape attached to it; form-filling is confusing and slow, and you must make an appointment and not just wander in. But having completed the formalities, remember that the solicitor is there to help you with your legal problems. Make sure that you get the service you are paying for.

Criminal Proceedings

The Civil Legal Aid Scheme does not apply to criminal cases, which are covered instead by the Criminal Legal Aid Scheme. If you have been charged with or wish to take a criminal case and you want legal aid, contact the court clerk of the court concerned.

How to Help your Solicitor to Help you

The law deals in facts. Emotions, suppositions and reactions, while of great relevance and personal concern to you, are not within its scope and the court, while appreciating your feelings, can make judgements only on facts.

Having found a solicitor who will handle your case, you arrive for an appointment. In order to save time and to help you over the initial stages of the interview, here is a checklist of information you can have already prepared, either writing it out with a copy to give to the solicitor or using it as a list of points to assist you and ensure that you give him/her all the necessary background information:

- full names and addresses of husband and wife
- age and religion of husband and wife
- date and place of marriage

- details of children: their names, dates of birth, sex, schools, etc.
- an up-to-date history of the marital relationship
- quality of relationship between parents and children
- financial details of husband and wife: jobs, incomes, housing situation
- details of immediate problem: custody, violence, maintenance, separation, etc.
- any other relevant information.

Your solicitor will need a copy of your marriage certificate and copies of the children's birth certificates. Never give a solicitor an original document of any kind; always get photocopies made and keep the originals in a safe place.

Solicitors' Costs

Looming almost as large as the problem which necessitates the visit to a solicitor is the question of cost. If you do not qualify for legal aid and are worried about money, ask. It is quite acceptable to ask your solicitor how much the consultations are going to cost; he/she should also be able to give you an estimate of what costs might be involved in taking a case to court. It is quite in order to offer to pay per visit rather than face a large bill at a future date. It is usual for solicitors to charge a fee in advance of taking a case, especially if litigation is involved. This is to ensure that you will proceed with your case. Some solicitors charge less than others, so shop around, if you can.

"Dirty Linen"

Your solicitor is going to need facts, dates, specific details and possible witnesses of violence or threats to you or the children, evidence of lack of support, persistent irresponsibility, cruelty, excessive drinking, infidelities or other behaviour such as would make life intolerable for you.

All this evidence will be scrutinised very carefully by the court and if the case is contested be prepared for a lot of public washing of dirty linen. The court is cleared for family law cases, that is, no one other than the parties, their legal representatives and the court staff may be present during the hearing. But to have your marital differences aired even before this small audience is a traumatic experience.

Many people feel that a court of law, however sympathetic, is no place in which to deal with marital disputes. Its adversarial approach and all the formalities—the seating arrangements, the rigid adherence to legal jargon and form of address, the uniformed police in the background—give the whole place an air of criminality that is alien and frightening to many people. It creates acute distress for both parties, who are already undergoing stress as a result of their marriage break-up.

Legal Terms—a Foreign Language?

The legal profession abounds with unwieldy, unfamiliar and unpronounceable terms and expressions, mostly utterly meaningless to lay people. Make sure that your solicitor explains the meaning of anything you do not fully understand. Do not feel intimidated or shy about asking; he/she is providing you with a service and it is important and right that you fully understand what is happening.

Going to the District Court

Courts are not the most pleasant of places. In fact, the condition of some District Courts is so bad that there have been newspaper reports of justices refusing to hear cases in them, due to their unheated, overcrowded and medieval state. For the most part they are gloomy and down-at-heel; in many cases there is no waiting-room or toilet facilities for clients. People must stand together outside the door of the court waiting for their case to be called, trying to consult with their solicitor while their spouse does likewise in another corner and the next three or four cases in line stand around waiting.

If you call to speak to the court clerk on business, you may have to talk through a hatch in a room where there is a client briefing a solicitor, several people with unpaid TV licences and possibly a parking offence or two, waiting. This is no place to be timid or shy. Stand your ground, state your case and make sure that the clerk understands what it is you want. Also, ensure that he or she makes a written note of any complaints or requests that need attention or reply. You may come out red-faced, mortified and gasping for air, but make sure that you get the service you went in for.

Which Court will Decide your Case?

If speed is important, some family cases are still best taken in the District Court. These include Maintenance and Barring and Protection Orders.

When dealing with family law cases, the circuit court is known as "the Circuit Family Court." The Circuit Family Court has now been empowered to determine proceedings under the Judicial Separation and Family Law Reform Act 1989 and the relevant related Acts (see page 92 for further details).

Several important changes have been made to the manner in which the court is conducted for these family cases. They are heard at different times to other cases, providing greater privacy in the corridors and waiting areas. The proceedings themselves in both the Circuit and the High Court are as informal as possible with neither the judges nor the barristers wearing wigs or gowns. All cases are held "in camera," that is, excluding anyone not connected with the case. The court will decide the costs of the case and who will pay them.

Your Legal Options

Barring and Protection Orders

Barring and Protection Orders were introduced to deal with family violence by protecting a spouse and/or children in the home where their safety or welfare is at risk from the other spouse.

A Barring Order means that the offending spouse is barred from entering the family home until the Order expires. Orders granted by the District Court are temporary, being granted for a period of from three to twelve months, while the Circuit Court can grant an indefinite Barring Order. According to the Family Law (Protection of Spouses and Children) Act, 1981, the District or Circuit Court may grant an Order "if it is of the opinion that there are reasonable grounds for believing that the safety or welfare of that spouse or of any child so requires." In effect, Barring Orders are rarely granted on grounds other than physical violence. However, see "Judicial Separation" on page 91 for remedies in non-violent situations.

To apply for a Barring Order, you can go to the court clerk at your local District Court (see the telephone directory under District Court). He/she will assist you in making an application. It is advisable to have legal representation at the actual court hearing. It takes about six to eight weeks for the case to come before the court. This is to allow time for your spouse to receive the summons to appear in court and to get legal representation.

On applying for the Barring Order, you can ask the court clerk about a Protection Order if you feel you or your children are in immediate physical danger. You will be asked, provided the judge is available, to state in your own words why you need the Order, furnishing proof where possible, and it will normally be granted on the spot. You do not need legal representation for this. The Protection Order does not remove the other spouse from the family home, but states that he/she shall not use or threaten to use violence, or molest or put in fear the applicant spouse or children before the hearing for the Barring Order.

If your spouse ignores the Protection Order and is violent, call the police. Under Section 7 of the Act, the police have powers of arrest without warrant for breaches of Barring or Protection Orders "at their discretion." The court will send a copy of such Orders to both spouses concerned and to the local Garda station.

In the meantime you can bring a copy of the Order to the station to make sure that the police are aware of the situation. A person who is convicted of breach of a Barring or Protection Order is liable to a fine not exceeding £200 or, at the discretion of the court, imprisonment for up to six months, or both.

Evidence from your doctor, priest or local police of any violence would be advisable to support your case. A letter may not suffice; the witnesses generally have to appear in court. If you have had to leave home because of violence you can still apply for a Barring Order. A barred spouse will have to leave the family home to allow you back into it. If the barred spouse wishes to have access to the children he/she can apply to the District or Circuit Courts which have the power to make orders relating to access or custody; the application can be made either at the hearing for barring or at a subsequent hearing.

If you cannot afford a solicitor, you can apply for legal aid at your nearest Legal Aid Centre. The charge for this is assessed according to your means and, in cases of extreme hardship, there may be no charge. In family law cases a wife is assessed on her own income, not her husband's. Housekeeping money is not regarded as income, but maintenance awarded by a court is. A man who is paying maintenance to his wife cannot deduct this from his income when being assessed for eligibility (see more on civil legal aid on page 76). You may choose not to get legal advice and to represent yourself; however, in the majority of cases this is not advisable.

When the barring period is over, your spouse may return to the family home. If necessary, you can apply for renewal of the Barring Order, though either spouse has the right to seek a discharge at any stage while Order is in operation. A Barring Order is not intended to be permanent. In the case of violence by a family member other than a spouse, you should inform your local police and social worker of what is happening. Where there is disagreement between the parents, you would need to seek legal advice.

Other legal remedies against a violent spouse or partner include applying for a Circuit or High Court injunction, or proceeding with an assault charge. The spouse can bring an assault charge if the police are reluctant to do so. These are criminal proceedings and Barring Orders were designed as a specific remedy under civil law for dealing with violent spouses.

You are Considering a Barring Order but Plan to Separate

If, either because your spouse is violent or for other reasons, you wish to separate legally, then it is much more efficient to take a case for Judicial Separation than to apply for a Barring Order. Under the Judicial Separation and Family Law Reform Act, 1989 you can apply for an Exclusion Order, excluding one spouse from the family home and granting the other spouse the sole right to reside there. This is not a Barring Order; it is granted only after a Judicial Separation. Violence does not necessarily have to be proven; behaviour which you consider to be intolerable and mental cruelty will be considered by the court. In granting an Exclusion Order, the court will take into account the welfare of the family as a whole and consider the position of the non-earning spouse and children now that the couple have decided to separate.

Separation Agreements

A separation agreement is exactly what it says: an agreement to separate and live apart, free from the marital control of the other spouse. It is based on a degree of co-operation between the spouses. The agreement can be verbal or written, but it is obviously better to have it in writing; and the contract (as it is called) is usually drawn up by a solicitor. A separation agreement, or Deed of Separation, is dependent on both spouses agreeing to the terms as set out in the agreement.

One great advantage to an agreement is that, if both parties are amenable, the contract can be drawn up and become operative within a relatively short time. There is no prescribed form of agreement; it can contain as many clauses as are relevant to the parties concerned. Most agreements contain clauses relating to:

- living apart
- non-molestation
- the matrimonial home
- custody and access of children
- maintenance.

It is generally thought to be in the interests of each party to have separate solicitors. The contents of the agreement have to be arrived at by negotiation between the parties, and having your own solicitor can best ensure that your wishes and needs are catered for within the agreement.

A separation agreement is a valid legal contract, and if either party fails to abide by its terms, the aggrieved spouse can enforce the agreement by taking the appropriate legal action. If, for example, the husband does not make the agreed maintenance payments, the wife may sue for breach of contract and obtain damages in respect of the arrears. Damages can also be awarded for failure to abide by any of the other terms of the agreement.

In any agreement or arrangement for maintenance, make sure that there is a cost of living clause included to keep pace with inflation. This will save legal costs, time and hassle later on.

A separation agreement does not entitle either party to remarry during the lifetime of the other spouse.

Mediation

Mediation is the art of making possible the seemingly impossible. The mediator is an impartial third party who can help a couple to resolve their conflicts and negotiate their own separation terms; this process encourages co-operation between the couple with the minimum of distress or bitterness.

Mediation is about **issues**, such as money, property, custody or access to the children. It is not counselling for feelings, although it can often alleviate the stress in a broken relationship by resolving some of the practical problems. With the help of the mediator, the couple can discuss and negotiate in an informal and confidential way those issues causing conflict, removed from the adversarial atmosphere of the courts or the law. With mediation it is possible to have consensus without the need for a "winner" or a "loser."

For this approach to work, both parties must agree to attend together and be prepared to discuss the contentious issue/s. The mediator acts as a referee, not as a judge; it is the couple themselves who arrive at the final agreement. The mediator can then help them draft their agreement, which is taken to their lawyers.

In my opinion, mediation should replace the existing court proceedings for family law cases. The family law courts should be so restructured that all cases coming before them have first been to mediation, with the court formally "rubber-stamping" the agreed arrangements. Only where consensus was not possible at mediation should a marital dispute face a full legal hearing.

There is now an excellent Government-funded family mediation service in Dublin whose assistance is free. Under the auspices of the Department of Justice, this was originally set up as a pilot scheme, but there is strong pressure from all professionals and voluntary organisations dealing with marital breakdown to retain and expand the service. For an appointment write to or ring the Secretary, Family Mediation Service, Irish Life Centre, Block 1, Floor 5, Lower Abbey Street, Dublin 1. There are several private organisations and individuals who also offer mediation. (See Appendix One.)

Judicial Separation

Divorce in Ireland is outlawed under Article 41 Section 3.2 of our Constitution: "No law shall be enacted providing for the grant of a dissolution of marriage."

However, you can apply to the courts for a Judicial (or Legal) Separation which allows you to live apart and makes legal provision for maintenance, custody, etc. Under the Judicial Separation and Family Law Reform

Act, 1989, you can apply for a Judicial Separation on one or more of the following grounds:

(a) that your spouse has committed adultery;

(b) that your spouse has behaved in such a way that you cannot reasonably be expected to live with him/her;

(c) that you have been deserted for a continuous period of at least one year immediately preceding the date of the application;

(d) that you and your spouse have lived apart from one another for a continuous period of at least one year immediately preceding the date of the application and your spouse consents to a decree being granted;

(e) that you and your spouse have lived apart from one another for a continuous period of at least three years immediately preceding the date of the application;

(f) that the marriage has broken down to the extent that the court is satisfied in all circumstances that a normal marital relationship has not existed between you and your spouse for a period of at least one year immediately preceding the date of application.

Where the court is satisfied that any of the above grounds has been proved on the balance of probabilities, the court shall grant a Decree of Judicial Separation. You are then legally separated but without the freedom to remarry as you are still legally married. Where there are dependent children, the court must be satisfied that adequate provision either has been made, or will be made when the Decree is granted.

One great advantage of this Act is that it is possible to take several related proceedings at one time. The court, before deciding whether or not to grant a Decree of Judicial Separation, may, if it appears to the court proper to do so, make any one or more of the following orders:

(a) a Barring or Protection order under the Family Law (Protection of Spouses and Children) Act, 1981 (see page 85);

(b) a Custody or Access Order or other order affecting the welfare of an infant under the Guardianship of Infants Act, 1964 (see page 101);

(c) an order for the protection of the family home, monies realised from it, household chattels or monies realised from their sale under the Family Home Protection Act, 1976 (see page 57).

Maintenance: On granting a decree of Judicial Separation or at any time thereafter the court may, on application to it by either spouse, make orders as to periodical payments, lump sums or regular payments to the other spouse and/or for the benefit of a dependent child of the family. While waiting for the case to come to court it is possible to apply to the court for maintenance pending suit, i.e. periodical payments to be paid to the dependent spouse and dependent child/children from the date of application to the court to the date of the determination of the case. Payments made on foot of an order of this Act can also be paid via the District Court clerk (see page 43).

Property: Orders can also be made regarding various transfers, settlements or sale of property as well as orders under various sections of the Married

Women's Status Act, 1957, the Family Home Protection Act, 1976 (see page 57) and the Partition Acts, 1868 and 1876.

Succession Rights: It is possible to apply to the court under the Judicial Separation and Family Law Reform Act, 1989 for an order extinguishing the share that your spouse might have in your estate under the Succession Act, 1965.

The court could, having considered the facts at the request of one spouse, make such an order if it was satisfied that adequate and reasonable provision had been made for the future security of the other spouse. See also "Succession of Children," page 194.

In deciding maintenance payments and property ownership the court takes into account:

- the income and property which each spouse has at present and is likely to have in the future;
- the financial needs and obligations which each has at present and is likely to have in the future;
- the standard of living enjoyed by the family up to the time of the separation;
- the age of each spouse, the length of time they were married, and the length of time they lived together;
- any physical or mental disability of either spouse;
- past and likely future contributions to the welfare of the family by either spouse—this includes financial and non-financial contributions;

94

- the effect of marital responsibilities on the earning capacity of each spouse, in particular the effect on the spouse who gave up career and earning opportunities to care for the family;
- income or benefits to which either spouse is legally entitled;
- conduct of either spouse which it would be unjust to ignore;
- accommodation needs of each spouse.

Other family law proceedings which can be dealt with by the Circuit Family Court include issues under the Adoption Acts, 1952 to 1988, the Legitimacy Declaration Act, (Ireland) 1868, and the Status of Children Act, 1987 (see page 99). Obviously, every detail of the various changes in legislation cannot be given here. Do consult a solicitor, a legal advice centre, or a legal aid board centre, or contact AIM Group. (See Appendix One for addresses.)

While the Judicial Separation and Family Law Reform Act, 1989 has wide-ranging provisions and allows a number of related matters to be dealt with at one time, it only goes as far as the Constitution will allow. You remain married to your spouse. You cannot get a divorce in Irish law; and are therefore not free to remarry. This may not bother you now. But at some point in the future you may wish to remarry, or at least have the option. You could seek a foreign divorce (see page 109) which might or might not be recognised in Irish law. It will require a successful outcome to another divorce referendum to alter Article 41 of our Constitution. In the meantime you must remain, however unwillingly, married to your spouse.

Application Procedure

Application for a Judicial Separation is made to the Circuit Court or the High Court, and is usually made through a solicitor. The solicitor will first ascertain that there are grounds to apply. He/she must then discuss with the client the possibility of reconciliation and supply names and addresses of persons suitably qualified to assist in this process. If this is ruled out, the solicitor must then raise the option of drawing up a mediated separation agreement, supplying names and addresses of qualified family mediators, and that of negotiating a written separation agreement. He/she must certify to the court that these possibilities have been investigated with the client.

The court can adjourn any application for a Decree before it, to give the spouses time to consider a reconciliation or, where it feels that a reconciliation is not possible, to give the spouses time to assess the terms of a separation agreement. The court may advise the assistance of a marriage counsellor or a family mediator in these matters. Discussions with a counsellor or mediator cannot be used as evidence in court.

Civil Decree of Nullity

This is the only civil action which can end a marriage currently available to married couples in Ireland. A decree of civil nullity states that no marriage has existed, even though a marriage ceremony has taken place. A marriage can be deemed to be either void or voidable.

Grounds Rendering a Marriage Void

A void marriage is one which is deemed never to have existed because of:

1. **Lack of Capacity**, which is where the parties go through a ceremony of marriage and
   (a) either party is at the time validly married to another person; or
   (b) the parties are within the prohibited degrees of relationship (related by blood or marriage); or
   (c) the parties are of the same biological sex.

2. **Non-Observance of Formalities** where the parties have married in knowing and wilful disregard of certain formal requirements relating to the marriage ceremony, such as in any place other than the church where the banns were published; without due notice to the registrar or without certificate of notice or licence from the registrar if necessary; in the absence of a registrar where such presence is necessary; in any place other than that specified in the Notice and Registrar's Certificate or in any certified Presbyterian Church without publication of banns or any licence.

3. **Absence of Consent** where a person's consent is either absent or extracted under pressure. Examples include insanity; intoxication; mistake and misrepresentation; the intention not to fulfil the fundamental terms of the marriage contract; and duress, intimidation and undue influence.

Grounds Rendering a Marriage Voidable

A voidable marriage is essentially a valid subsisting marriage until a decree of annulment is granted, the parties to that marriage having brought nullity proceedings.

Impotence is a ground if it existed at the time of the marriage and if it results in non-consummation of the marriage. This includes physical inability stemming from psychological causes. Depending on the circumstances of the case, wilful refusal to consummate a marriage may or may not be a ground.

Inability to Enter Into and Sustain a Normal Marriage Relationship is also a ground for a decree of nullity. Before 1982 there was no precedent in Irish law for granting a decree on this ground. In a case that year, (R.S.J. v. J.S.J.), a decree of annulment was sought on the basis that the petitioner allegedly suffered from schizophrenia or some similar illness, and was as a result "incapable of contracting a valid marriage because he was so ill that he was unable to maintain and sustain a normal relationship with his wife." That particular case was refused as the Justice was not satisfied that on the date of his marriage the petitioner was so incapacitated as to make the marriage void or voidable.

A further case (D. v. C.) succeeded in the application when the petitioner was able to establish that the respondent "suffered from a manic depressive illness which was present throughout the duration of his relationship with the petitioner both before, at the time of and after their marriage" (from *Family Law in the Republic of Ireland* by Alan Shatter, see Appendix Two).

Subsequently several civil decrees of nullity have been granted where there was no allegation of mental illness but where it could be proved that a person lacked

98

the ability or capacity to enter into and sustain a normal marital relationship. In a 1989 case (P.C. v. J.C.) a decree of nullity was granted because of the emotional immaturity or "lack of capacity" of both parties and because they had entered into marriage unaware of the fact that they would find it impossible to sustain a normal relationship (from *The Irish Times* "Law Report," 2/10/89).

Further information or details on civil annulments should be sought from a solicitor. The above-mentioned book by Alan Shatter is a useful reference book on the subject. The whole question of the interpretation of the different grounds, how to apply, the cost of taking a case to the High Court, the legal, social and financial consequences of being granted a decree of nullity are all matters best considered with a solicitor well briefed with the details of your marital history. Once granted a civil decree of nullity, you would be eligible for Unmarried Mother's Allowance if you have children, but not for Deserted Wife's Payment or a Widow's Pension.

The Status of Children

The Status of Children Act, 1987 came into effect on 14 June, 1988. Its aim was to abolish the legal concept of illegitimacy and to establish the principle of equal rights for all children born within or outside marriage. Some differences remain, especially in the area of the rights of unmarried fathers. The law on adoption is only incidentally affected by this Act and distinctions between children born inside and outside marriage are central to that law.

In theory, the abolition of the concept of illegitimacy should mean that it would no longer be necessary, in law or practice, to distinguish between marital and non-marital children. In practice, the concept is not entirely abolished so it is sometimes necessary to so distinguish. Children who used to be referred to as "illegitimate" are now referred to as "children whose parents have not married each other."

The Act does bring major changes in the areas of guardianship, maintenance and succession. The term "illegitimate" is no longer used.

Subsequent Marriage of the Single Mother

You can alter your child's legal position if you marry the father at any time after the birth. The father then has automatic guardianship rights (see "Guardianship" below). However, the baby must be reregistered, giving the new details.

If the mother marries someone other than the father, her husband has no rights or duties as regards that child. The natural father would still be liable for maintenance. The married couple could apply to adopt the child and, if successful, they would have all the rights and duties, the natural father losing his rights and his obligations to maintain. If the natural father had become a guardian, his consent to the adoption would be required.

Guardianship and Custody of Children

Guardianship bestows parents with rights and duties in respect of the upbringing of their children. Parents have, for instance, a duty to maintain and provide for their children and the right to make decisions regarding them: for example, as to their education. Someone other than one of the child's parents can be the guardian. You can, for example, appoint by deed or will or through the courts a person to be your child's guardian, either in your absence or in the event of your death.

Custody is different, legally, in that it is the right to actual care and control on a day-to-day basis. A parent deprived of custody may still have a say in the upbringing of that child, remaining a guardian.

Husband and wife are joint guardians of their children and retain joint guardianship even if they separate and cease to live together. However, custody is usually given to one parent with access to visit given to the other. This does not necessarily have to be a legal decision arrived at through court proceedings. In many, probably most, cases, one parent either continues to live in the home with the children, the other parent leaving, or else one parent leaves the family home taking the child/children. In these instances, where usually it is the wife who keeps the children (especially if they are young), she has day-to-day responsibility, care and control and the husband is bound to maintain them, usually allowed visiting rights and access and entitled to be consulted on decisions relating to education, religion and suchlike.

Joint Custody has become quite a popular option with American courts in custody cases. Parents share the custody and daily care of their children, sometimes on a week-on week-off basis, or perhaps on a monthly or six-monthly basis, with the children moving between homes or occasionally the parents moving between homes to take up their stint as the carer for the period. In theory this keeps both parents interested and involved in the sharing and caring of the upbringing of their children and allows the children ready access to both parents on a more "natural" level than the usual visitation arrangements. However, it requires a deep level of commitment from both parents to their parental responsibilities, a good inter-parental communication system and the ability, financial and otherwise, to set up two suitable homes in reasonable proximity to each other. Also, how do the children feel about being shunted from one home to the other at regular intervals, having to duplicate possessions and having their routine and personal and social lives disrupted in this way? It would still appear to be the opinion of Irish courts and judges that children from broken marriages need to establish roots and should not be moved constantly from parent to parent. However, private separation agreements may well provide for joint custody if the parents so wish it.

Guardianship Proceedings

Since the Status of Children Act, 1987, the mother of a child born outside marriage remains the sole guardian but the father may acquire guardianship rights. Unmarried fathers do not have the same rights as married fathers. There are still legal distinctions between children born within marriage and those born outside marriage. Fathers in civilly annulled marriages now have the same rights as married fathers.

How the Father can Become a Joint Guardian

In order to become a joint guardian the father must acquire a court order. There are two ways to get this:

1. If the mother agrees to his being a joint guardian and the father's name is on the Register of Births (see "Registering the Baby's Birth" below) then he can apply for a court order using a simple and informal court procedure.

2. If the mother does not agree or if the father is not on the Register, then a full formal hearing is required.

In all guardianship cases, the decision is made on the basis that the welfare of the child is the first and paramount consideration. The father has the right to apply to the court for guardianship; he does not have an automatic right to guardianship itself. The rights of an unmarried father in a stable relationship would be considered by the courts to be greater than the rights of an unmarried father where the child was conceived as a result of a casual liaison. If the father becomes a joint guardian, then he has the usual guardianship rights, including the right to consent to or refuse an adoption.

Registering the Baby's Birth

Where a baby is born in hospital, the usual practice is for the hospital to register the birth. However, this does not have to be the case; the parent or parents can register the birth themselves.

If the parents are not married (or are not married to each other) the hospital will register only the mother's name. If you want to register both parents:

- ■ you can both go together to the local Registrar's office and register the birth or

- ■ one of you can go there bringing either a statutory declaration by the other parent and, if you are married, one signed by your husband to say that he is not the child's father; or a court order naming the man as the father of the child. The latter can be either an order giving the father guardianship rights or a Maintenance Order (or old Affiliation Order). With a court order, the other parent's consent to having the father's name on the Register is unnecessary.

Declaration of Parentage

The question of paternity is determined when you go to court for guardianship, maintenance or property proceedings. If you do not wish to take any of these proceedings you can apply to the Circuit Court for a declaration of paternity. This is not available to adopted children.

Blood Tests

The Status of Children Act, 1987 provides that the court in any proceedings where paternity is in question may order blood tests. The court may draw inferences from a refusal to have a test.

What you Need to Know if Considering Taking a Custody Action

■ You must be already living apart from your spouse before a custody action can come into force.

■ If a Custody Order has been made and the couple live together for a continuous period of three months or more at any time after it is made, it will cease to have effect.

■ If you left your spouse, you will want to be able to establish that you had substantial grounds (see "Constructive Desertion," page 44); you must also show that you can provide a stable home for the children and will be able to raise and educate them properly.

■ The court can order the spouse who does not get custody to pay maintenance towards the upkeep of the children, but it can make no Maintenance Order for the other spouse unless separate proceedings are brought under the Family Law (Maintenance of Spouses and Children) Act, 1976, or the Judicial Separation and Family Law Reform Act, 1989.

■ An award of custody is never final. The other parent is free at any time to apply to the court for a variation of the terms of custody; for example, with regard to access or his/her right of guardianship on matters such as schooling or religion.

■ If the other parent is concerned about the physical or moral welfare of the child/children, he/she can seek the direction of the court on matters where the parents cannot agree for themselves.

What is Best for the Child?

In custody cases the court does not act as a referee. To quote Justice Kenny on a case in 1971, "An award of custody is not a prize for good matrimonial behaviour." Section 3 of the Guardianship of Infants Act, 1964 obliges the court to "regard the welfare of the infant as the first and paramount consideration," this welfare comprising the "religious and moral, intellectual, physical and social welfare of the infant." (An infant is a child up to sixteen years of age.) However, this principle is not at all clear when you follow the actual cases.

A decision in any particular case will depend on the circumstances of the case and on the opinion of the presiding judge as to what, in these circumstances, best serves the welfare of the child or children. One of the most important aspects to be considered by the court will be why and how your marriage broke down. The behaviour and character of each of the parents will be taken into account when assessing suitability as custodian of the children. Many of the rulings have hinged on the extra-marital sexual activities of the parents with judgements on custody being weighted heavily on the basis of the moral (or immoral) behaviour of one of the parents. In a country with no divorce facility, the likelihood of extra-marital relationships is bound to increase, with subsequent difficulties for custody cases and the application of the "welfare" principle.

The other prime considerations of the court will be the ages of the children, their sex, their relationship with each other, whether they live at home, go to boarding-school or are in care, what type of family environment they live in and, in the case of older children, their own stated preferences as to with which parent they wish to live. Occasionally, the judge will request a meeting with the children, not in court but in his room. He/she will not necessarily ask them direct questions but, by talking to them, will be able to get a better picture of the family relationship.

Who Gets Custody?

This will depend on the particulars of each case but, as a general rule, custody of young children, and, in the case of older children, custody of daughters, is usually given to the mother. Sometimes the court will give custody to the mother until the children reach a certain age, and then require that custody be transferred to the father or, more commonly, that the matter be reconsidered at that stage.

In situations where there is very little difference as to which parent is more suitable, or where each parent lacks, to some degree, the proper characteristics of a suitable custodian, the court will have to decide what is in the best interests of the child. Where the court grants a Decree of Judicial Separation under the Judicial Separation and Family Law Reform Act, 1989, it may declare either spouse to be unfit to have custody of any dependent child of the family. Where a decree contains such a declaration then this parent shall not, on the death of the other, be entitled as of right to the custody of that child.

Where one parent is cohabiting or living in adultery this has, as I mentioned above, posed particular

107

difficulties for the court in its decisions. The adulterous parent is unlikely to be granted custody, but judgements vary. The court will study in great detail the particular circumstances of each case in order to assess not only the suitability of each parent with regard to custody, but also what circumstances best serve the welfare of the child. Obviously, the court would take into account such things as addictions to drugs, alcohol, gambling, mental stability and the home environment of both parties.

If you have been granted custody and your spouse at any time fails to fulfil the imposed obligations—for instance, to abide by the agreed visiting arrangements—you can take the case back to court, if the matter cannot be settled amicably between you. Of course, it would be much better for all concerned and also much quicker and cheaper if you can settle your differences without recourse to the courts each time. A mediator or a good solicitor will (or should) do all in his/her power to solve your legal wrangles for you without the financial and emotional cost of going to court, though co-operation and some degree of compromise will be essential. The traumatic upheaval of a series of court cases should usually be avoided and, in custody disputes, there are no winners, only losers. See "Mediation," page 90.

Domicile

Your domicile is your legal residence, that place where you are permanently residing or will permanently reside. It is not necessarily the place in which you are now living.

Domicile and Recognition of Foreign Divorces Act, 1986

An important change in legislation since the earlier (1982) edition of this book pertains to the domicile of married women, whereby a married woman now retains her own domicile, independent of her husband. The 1986 Act also affects the domicile of minors.

The Act provides that, where the parents are living apart and the child has her home with her mother and no home with her father, the child will have her mother's domicile. If the child's domicile has been with her mother and she dies and the child has not since had a home with her father, she will continue to be legally regarded as domiciled in her mother's place of domicile.

On the recognition of foreign divorces, the Act rules that the divorce shall be recognised if it is granted in the country where either spouse is domiciled. To be domiciled you have to have residency in the State granting the divorce, but increasing numbers of people are being granted foreign divorces using residency addresses.

The residency requirement applies to divorces granted after the Act came into force—2 October, 1986. The recognition of divorces granted before that time will depend on the previous law, whereby a married woman automatically had the domicile of her husband. Under that law, if a husband became domiciled in another State he could apply for and be granted a divorce, without his wife ever leaving Ireland. But a wife whose husband remained in Ireland could not seek a separate domicile abroad.

Article 41 Section 3.3 of our Constitution states that:

> No person whose marriage has been dissolved under the civil law of any other State but is a subsisting valid marriage under the law for the time being in force within the jurisdiction of the Government and Parliament established by this Constitution shall be capable of contracting a valid marriage within that jurisdiction during the lifetime of the other party to the marriage so dissolved.

Many people applying for British or other foreign divorces are not too concerned with Article 41 of our Constitution. Their marriage has broken down, they wish to be free of its legally restraining bonds and they may or may not wish to remarry. Will their foreign divorce be recognised in Irish law?

There is no clear answer. The Department of Social Welfare and the Revenue Commissioners will recognise a foreign divorce for social welfare and tax purposes. But if its legality is challenged in the courts, especially under wills or inheritance questions, no one is yet sure how the foreign divorce will stand up. The danger here is that, by then, the person granted the divorce may have remarried and have a second family which may or may not be recognised under Irish law. Only if domicile has been seen to have been established elsewhere will the divorce be recognised by the Irish courts.

There are several grounds under which recognition of the foreign divorce may be withheld by the court. These are fraud, duress and the denial of justice (collusion would be an example of the latter). The ground most likely to cause concern is fraudulent invocation of jurisdiction, i.e. pretending to have domicile in the

110

requisite State in order to be granted a divorce. This could be contested in an Irish court and recognition could be withheld from a foreign decree of divorce.

It may prevent some inheritance problems later if the couple draw up a separation agreement before applying for divorce. This agreement could include a clause renouncing succession rights for the spouses, but would not affect the children's rights. Anyone planning a second marriage (or live-in relationship) should make a will in favour of the new spouse/partner as this will provide a measure of protection.

If your Spouse Divorces you

If you have received a letter from a solicitor in England or elsewhere telling you that your spouse has petitioned for divorce, and you are not happy about this, take the letter along to your solicitor, to your legal aid centre or to AIM Group. If there is none of these agencies near you, a chat with a clergyman or social worker may help you to decide calmly how to handle the problem. Be aware that this can be a very traumatic moment, conclusively heralding the end to the marriage.

If your spouse is applying to an English court for a divorce and you wish to oppose this, you could write to The Law Society (see Appendix One for address) for a list of solicitors in whatever region of England your spouse's solicitor's letter came from. You can choose one and write to him/her giving the name of your spouse's solicitor. He or she should be able to advise you as to what you must do; whether you need to go to England for the hearing and whether you would qualify for English legal aid.

If your spouse obtains a foreign divorce which is recognised in Ireland, then you can remarry in Ireland or anywhere else. If, however, your former spouse has lived all his/her married life overseas, but with the intention of returning to Ireland, then he/she may retain an Irish domicile and the Irish courts may not recognise this divorce, even though he/she was resident in an overseas jurisdiction at the time of the decree being granted.

Changing your Name—Reverting to your Maiden Name

You can change your name by deed poll or simply by informing everyone with whom you deal that you wish to be called by another name. You can revert to your maiden name, take your new partner's name or any other, with no formalities, but you must obtain your husband's consent if you wish your children to take your name instead of his. There is no legal requirement to take your husband's name on marriage, this is merely a social convention. If you do decide to change your name, do notify your bank and insurance company and check any legal documents you may have, particularly your will.

Church Annulments

Hundreds of Irish men and women are in the ambiguous and anomalous situation of having been granted a **decree of nullity** by a Marriage Tribunal of the Roman Catholic Church, although their marriages are held to be valid by the State. The whole area of a Church annulment and its practical consequences are often a muddle of confusion and incomprehension.

People will comment, "Now you have your Church annulment you are free to marry again." As far as the Church is concerned, they are correct. The Church has found that the marriage you contracted was not a true marriage for whatever reasons, has declared it null and void (never to have existed) and now views you as single.

But you also got married civilly and only a **civil decree of nullity** (see page 96) will leave you legally single once more, and permitted in law to remarry.

A Church annulment is an official pronouncement by the Roman Catholic Church about **the marriage at the time of its celebration**, so the procedure is of little use to those marriages which were quite normal, healthy and happy for a number of years and broke down only because of circumstances which arose at a later date. Church annulments are available only to Roman Catholics; the Anglican, Presbyterian, Methodist and Jewish faiths do not have a similar procedure.

The procedures for handling applications used to be long and complicated, but have been streamlined over the last twenty years, in principle making application and processing easier and quicker. However, cases are dealt with on a first come, first served basis which means that a complicated case could hold up the cases following it, causing delays.

According to a spokesman in the Dublin Regional Tribunal, there has been no increase in the number of people applying over the last decade. Approximately 650 to 700 applications are received each year. There has been a slight rise in the number of cases being processed each year due to an increase in staff. On average one application in six to seven cases is successful.

Do you have Grounds for a Church Annulment?

The grounds for a Church annulment are quite different from those for a Judicial Separation. What counts in a Church annulment are certain conditions or personality disorders which exist **at the time of the marriage** and which subsequently have a detrimental effect on the marriage that will make it void or voidable. The Tribunal does not consider behaviour during the course of the marriage which makes life intolerable for the other spouse, unless this behaviour stems from an illness or disorder which existed when the marriage took place.

The three broad headings under which a Church annulment can be granted are: the existence of an impediment, failure to observe the proper formalities, and defective consent.

The impediments to marriage include being under age, impotence, a previous valid marriage, blood relationship, holy orders, and solemn religious vows.

The proper formalities require that a marriage takes place before an authorised priest and two witnesses.

Defective consent is the area most exercised in applications for annulment. Consent freely given is essential to marriage. If either or both parties get married with the intention of excluding some or all of the essential elements, then their consent is defective

114

and the marriage invalid as a result. The essential elements are: permanence, faithfulness, and sexual intercourse which can lead to conception. Thus, if one of the couple has decided at the time of marriage that he/she does not want children or does not regard fidelity as a part of marriage, the partner could apply for an annulment.

The Church authorities were quicker than the State to recognise that there are psychological reasons why a marriage cannot work for some people. Canon law classifies as follows certain people as incapable of contracting a valid marriage:

- those who lack sufficient use of reason;
- those who suffer from a grave lack of discretion of judgement concerning the essential matrimonial rights and obligations to be mutually given and accepted;
- those who, because of causes of a psychological nature, are unable to assume the essential obligations of marriage.

(From *Nullity of Marriage in the Catholic Church,* by the Catholic Press & Information Office.)

The whole concept of "psychological incapacity" involves the evidence and expertise of psychologists and psychiatrists.

In about 75 per cent of nullity cases granted by the Catholic Church in Ireland, one or both parties are prohibited from entering into another marriage without the special permission of the local bishop. This is to prevent the sacrament of marriage being brought into disrepute, and it also protects the interests of a future spouse.

If you are not sure whether you have grounds for a Church annulment, the Catholic Marriage Advisory Council (see phone book for local centres) may be able to help you; alternatively you could just apply and discuss it with the Tribunal.

How to Apply for a Church Annulment

You can approach the priest in your parish, explain that you wish to apply for an annulment, and seek his assistance. This may be a good idea for several reasons. Firstly, he will know the correct procedure and may even offer to write to the Tribunal on your behalf, if you find this a daunting task. Secondly, as your parish priest or curate, it is possible that he knows you and your spouse personally and, if so, he may know or suspect that there are problems in the marriage. This knowledge could be of considerable importance to the Tribunal when assessing your case.

There are four regional Tribunals: Armagh, Cork, Dublin and Galway. You address your letter to The Administrator. The Dublin Regional Marriage Tribunal address is: Archbishop's House, Drumcondra, Dublin 9. Tel: (01) 379253. The other addresses will be in the telephone book. Write to the Regional Tribunal, stating your case briefly and concisely, and requesting an interview.

After Applying—What Next?

Be prepared to wait quite a long time before you hear anything; remember that each case is dealt with in order of application. If the delay seems unreasonably long or you are worried that they may have forgotten you, a short note or a telephone call will usually suffice. They are probably working on your case but not keeping you informed.

The Cost of an Annulment

The cost of a Church annulment is very modest compared to the costs of any civil legal action. The present sum requested is £400, which has not increased since 1986. This charge applies irrespective of how long the case takes from initial application to final decision. If the parties cannot afford it, they are asked to pay what they can afford, and in some cases the fee can be waived.

A case will usually take between one and three years from start to finish. A civil nullity case in the High Court, lasting perhaps two to four days, could cost thousands of pounds, including the many months of preparation and the fees of solicitors and barristers.

Confidentiality

Church annulment proceedings offer total confidentiality throughout. At no time during the three years it took my case to be granted did I meet anyone other than my case-worker. Even on the morning of the hearing, when my husband and several nominated witnesses were called, I arrived, gave my evidence to the Tribunal and left, meeting no other person connected with my case. Thus, there were no awkward moments, no embarrassing or bitter exchanges, no possibility of upset at a time when nerves are naturally fraught and tensions run high. I found this confidentiality very reassuring and while three years is a long time to await an important decision in your life, the privacy afforded to the details of the case did compensate for the delay.

Religious and Social Reasons for wanting an Annulment

In a predominantly Catholic country, it is probably not surprising that a lot of people find it reassuring to receive acknowledgement from their Church of their changed status. In the same way as they wished for their Church's blessing on their wedding day, they now want her official acknowledgement that the marriage no longer exists. In fact, in the Church's view, it never existed.

It must also be said that, in the absence of divorce legislation, a separated person is deemed more socially "acceptable" if he or she has the **imprimatur** of the Church. Hypocritical though it may be, the fact remains that a Church annulment is seen as more respectable than plain separation. In a society which has to categorise people into little boxes, annulled is a box above deserted or separated. The fact that it has no bearing on the legal validity of the marriage is an irony ignored or misunderstood by most. A falling away in the faith of many separated people, who feel alienated and rejected by their Church, clergy and fellow-worshippers, is changing this as people make their own arrangements for their personal lives, without deference to Church or State.

Married or Not?

The fact that your marriage is annulled by the Roman Catholic Church is not recognised in civil law; nor are the grounds on which it is granted. Furthermore, the fact that you have a Church annulment does not mean you are in a better position to seek a civil annulment. Your marriage is still in existence as far as the State is concerned and the Church annulment does not affect the status of your children, your inheritance entitlements to your spouse's property, or your entitlements as a spouse to social welfare. If you remarry during the lifetime of your spouse you could face bigamy charges. Any maintenance or custody provisions must be sought separately under civil law.

5

Children

How They Cope

The National Children's Bureau in Britain maintains that it is poverty and all its associated problems which puts many children in one-parent families at a disadvantage, and not the fact of their being brought up by just one parent. In Britain, single-parent families make up almost half of all families living in poverty.

> The number of one-parent families is growing in Ireland, as elsewhere. By 1986 the number of one-parent families had grown to over 97,000, making up 10% of all private households in Ireland...between one-quarter and one-third of all families worldwide are supported by women and these families have been found to be leading candidates for poverty and hardship. One of the main reasons why one-parent families have both a high risk of being poor and of staying poor is because they are denied access to the most effective route out of poverty: full-time employment for both parents.

(from *Women and Poverty* by Mary Daly.)

According to Article 41 of our Constitution, "The State guarantees to protect the family in its constitution and authority, as the necessary basis of social order and as indispensable to the welfare of the Nation and the State." However, the State makes only half-hearted and piecemeal efforts at providing for its most vulnerable group of families, the one-parent families.

> Families headed by a woman on her own are becoming increasingly reliant on social welfare. The number of women claiming "deserted wife's" payments, for instance, has doubled over the past ten years. Some mothers on their own have difficulty in getting maintenance from the State. The conditions attaching to "women's schemes" (i.e. "deserted wife," "unmarried mother," "widow," "single woman," "prisoner's wife") can be difficult to satisfy.

(from *Women and Poverty*).

It would appear that while the State gives, it gives very grudgingly, almost reluctantly and, in so doing, embarrasses and degrades recipients.

Priests and so-called "protect the family" groups expound from the altar and in public on the delinquency of the children (and indeed parents) of broken homes; as though the children of two-parent families were all upstanding citizens and those from broken homes a lesser breed. And in the middle of all this there are lone parents conscientiously rearing families, trying to make ends meet, trying to live normal lives, and doing so not only unaided by Church or State but often in spite of them. I will give just one personal example. In 1986, coming up to the divorce referendum, the local parish priest delivered a sermon that was gratuitously offensive to those whose marriages had broken down, referring to the "evil that could stalk the land and threaten our families, the evil of divorce." It appeared that we were a threat to them and had to be cut out like a canker. I was so upset by it that I made an appointment and went to see him to ask why he had been so hurtful and insulting. He was totally taken aback. He said he was sure that there were "few, if any" such families (separated or deserted) in the parish but declined my offer to meet some. He was genuinely ignorant of a whole facet of family life in the community around him.

Lone parents have more than enough real live problems without being made to feel guilty for a way of life that, in most cases, is not of our choosing. Very few of us opt to go it alone; any choice is definitely of the Hobsonian variety: the lesser of two evils. To choose that road and travel it, with little or no official recognition or support, with censure from the Church and suspicion from society, is hard indeed. Lone parents deserve medals for courage and achievements in the face of this opposition; opposition, I might add, from the people who purport to uphold Article 41 of the Constitution.

Fears and Problems

First of all, it is important to stress that, while children of lone parents present problems, children with two parents also have problems, for example, petty stealing, bed-wetting, learning difficulties, mitching from school, and so on. It must be made clear that ordinary, straightforward problems: are not exclusively lone-parent-related. The professionals—teachers, doctors, psychologists—may try to use your marital status to explain away whatever problems may arise. Insist that the problem be investigated and not written off as inevitable in your situation.

There are studies which show that family discord is associated with antisocial problems in childhood (for example, see Rutter's *Parent-Child Separation— Psychological Effects on the Child*). However, Rutter suggests that this association applies to homes which have not been broken by divorce, death or separation, and his theory is that it is the unhappiness of the strained marital relationship which is the relevant factor. This theory is supported by others. J.M. Kauffman (in *Characteristics of Children's Behavioural Disorders*, see Appendix Two) suggests that, in an intact family, parental discord may exert a more pernicious influence than impending or actual separation. Rutter also states that, where marital discord coexists with poverty, illness, poor housing, parental violence and unemployment, the effects multiply. In other words, where two such factors occur together, this more than doubles the probability that the child will develop a behavioural disorder. As the factors increase, so do the problems for the child (see "Marital Adjustment and Behaviour Problems in Children" by C. Lucey and M. Fitzgerald, *Irish Journal of Medical Science*, November 1989). In essence, it is marital discord, not separation, which can cause many children's behavioural problems.

Problems displayed by the children of lone parents may be no worse than those displayed by two-parented children but the lone parent may find those problems much more difficult to cope with. Lack of time, money, education, confidence; not knowing whom to turn to for help; having no one with whom to share the worry of the problem; all these build up and can create a vicious circle of child-parent-child problems.

No one will deny that a parent disappearing through death, desertion, or violence in the home has a disturbing effect on a child. How the remaining parent responds to the situation is very important in helping the child to cope. Children, even within the one family, will react differently, depending on their relationships with their parents, their own personal level of security, the support they receive at the time of the break-up, and many other factors.

The American experience is that divorce is a different experience for children and adults because children lose the family structure that is fundamental to their development. When that structure collapses, the children's world is temporarily without supports. Children do not want their parents to separate, even if they know they are very unhappy together. Whatever shortcomings family life may have, the child's security comes from the "known," and family breakdown, separation and divorce are unknown and therefore to be feared.

Children's reactions differ at these times, some becoming clinging and very dependent, some "bold" and difficult to manage, seeking attention, while others "switch off" and express minimal interest in anything. Others may blossom, removed, perhaps, from the arena of violence, abuse or alcoholism. These children see the fear leave the remaining parent and relax accordingly.

124

As a rule, I would worry most about the child who switches off. Here's why. When life is tense or a constant struggle against deprivation, children can become apathetic or frustrated. On becoming a lone parent, you are going to be so busy, so rushed, so concerned about money, your home, how to cope, the loneliness, the isolation and all the demands and pressures on you, that the child who is quiet and retires to her room or just sits passively, unquestioningly, making no demands on your time or emotional reserves, will appear a godsend. You may even remark to friends how good she is. But that child, just as much as the clinging or difficult one, is crying out for reassurance, love, attention and affection. The others are asking for it in their own way; she cannot. Spend time, make time, give as much of yourself as you possibly can to reassuring the children that they are loved and wanted. Make sure they realise that they are blameless and not, as many children fear, the cause of the break-up. Children cannot rationalise very well, particularly younger ones, and they see no reason to suppose that now one parent has left or died, the other one will not go also.

While you are trying to cope with the hurt and trauma of the death of a spouse, marital breakdown, or unmarried pregnancy, children are not going to be just a source of joy. You are going to be frightened and overburdened by the task, and resent them because their emotional and practical demands intrude on the massive job you have coping with your problems. How can you give them love when no one is loving you or helping you? You can, but it is not always going to be easy.

You must realise that the children need to grieve their absent parent and the end of the family. Their pain, grief and fear may or may not relate to or match how you feel, but their whole world has just come apart and they do not understand or want to accept the changed circumstances.

So, while you feel that you are greatly in need of love and understanding yourself, you must give it unstintingly to your child. It will repay you a thousandfold and very quickly, because, as the child gains confidence and balance in her new world, the bond between you will strengthen. In time you will discover that children are generous in giving affection and will provide you with a morale boost when your flagging spirits need it most.

How to Answer their Questions

This is one area where the widow/widower has an easier, more straightforward task than the parent who is separated, deserted, unmarried or whatever. If mummy/daddy has died, there are firstly and obviously all the trappings of mourning and grief: the funeral, the letters and flowers of sympathy, the tears and the support of family and friends. If the child is included in all that is happening, she will have time to understand a little and accept the loss of a parent. We can pray for mummy/daddy who has gone to live with God and who is very happy and thinking of us all the time. We may perhaps occasionally visit the grave and place favourite flowers there. All of this ritual will help the child to cope with her loss.

But for the child whose parent has left home, or worse, the child who must flee the family home leaving behind not only one parent but all that is familiar and a part of her, this surely is a traumatic experience. Here there is no period of mourning and no obvious reason for all the upset. There may be bitter exchanges and recriminations on both sides, or haggling over who owns what or what each partner is entitled to. The child may hear rows and discussions about "who gets the children" as though they were pots and pans, and may really fear that no one wants her at all, that she may get left or given away, like the old clothes.

The rule is: be honest. For the younger child it is usually sufficient to say that mum and dad were not happy being together and so dad (or mum) is going to live in a different house and then everyone will be happier. If the separation is final, do not hint or imply that there is a chance you will all be back together soon. Children can be quite philosophical and will probably believe and accept what you tell them—even if they do not agree with what you say! Therefore, keep it simple, straight and honest. Try not to apportion blame or to criticise the absent parent.

Having said that, it must be recognised that you are going to say negative things about the partner in a marriage break-up. Your attitude as much as what you actually say will make it fairly clear how you feel. Do not feel guilty about this, it is human and normal. But do not expect your children to share your feelings; they may be very attached to their other parent and love him/her dearly.

If you have separated and your spouse has visiting rights (see "Custody of Children," page 101), try to ensure that he/she visits on a regular basis and, most importantly, that when your husband/wife arranges to come on a certain day at a certain time, this arrangement is adhered to. It is utterly soul-destroying and wrecking to watch a child gazing out of the window, asking every minute, "What time is it now? He will be here soon, won't he? He promised."

As the children get older, it may be possible to explain to them simply that, while you would very much like to be a "proper" family, for various reasons it was not possible; and that, while you do realise that they miss their father, living with one parent in harmonious surroundings is preferable to living with two who are constantly rowing or waging silent but bitter warfare.

The children may feel that it is their duty to try to mend the marriage, or that the welfare of either the absent or the remaining parent (or both) is now their responsibility. Because two parents and the family unit are all the children have ever known, they are going to try, either consciously or subconsciously, to reconstruct it, and will feel very guilty or powerless when they do not succeed.

Not all children ask direct questions; a child who does not ask about her father may miss him just as keenly as one who does. So do not wait for the direct questions. Fill in the grey areas for them, rather than leaving them with a vacuum which may get filled with fears or distorted images. If you cannot think of much good to say about the absent parent, at least do not say anything bad. Your husband, however you may feel about him, is the child's father. Try to keep a positive image of him in the child's mind, so that she can grow up accepting her absent parent and not judging or condemning him. Remember that, while your marriage did not survive, that does not mean that either partner, as a person, is a failure.

Do not be surprised if, after many years of separation, as the children reach their mid-teens or adulthood, they seek out the absent parent. They may wish to verify their own opinions and feelings and they may need to see their "other half." After all, they come from two parents; they may resemble in appearance or personality the absent parent, wish to see that parent and establish a connection. If there has been little or no contact between your spouse and yourself, this may be a difficult period. Your children may return from visits unhappy, confused or angry. They may receive conflicting and upsetting information from the other parent, or challenge your authority or the reasons you gave for the break-up. They may be offered financial or other inducements to remain with or spend more time with the other parent, making family life competitive and combative. They may be encouraged or introduced to entertainments inappropriate to their ages, such as pubs, night-clubs or drugs, which may well attract but confuse them. Your intervention will be interpreted as "fuddy-duddy," boring and childish with a glamorous alternative life-style being proffered. Talk to them. Seek help, professional or otherwise, if you cannot tackle it alone. Be honest in letting them know that you do not have all the answers or solutions, but that you do have their welfare and happiness at heart. They may choose, even if only for a while, to live with the other parent against your judgement or wishes. Let them know that you care and are there at any time should they need you. If you fear they may be in danger or involved in illegal activities, do not be afraid to call the police.

Some Behaviour Problems

Attention-Seeking

This may present itself in many ways, such as bad behaviour and disobedience. It is most upsetting for the lone parent since you feel you are losing control and cannot cope. To start with, we are probably more sensitive as lone parents in an effort to prove that we can manage. We may over-react and worry about problems which are, in most cases, just a part of the child growing up. While a degree of discipline must be maintained and certain rules adhered to, what this child needs is tons of your affection and time. Her naughtiness is often a cry for reassurance that you still love her and need her, that she is not just another of your problems. If she is good you can get on with your work, but by being naughty she can make you very much aware of her presence: hence the bad behaviour. Leave the dishes or the beds unmade and read a story, play a game or go for a walk with her. Take the time to put her to bed properly, with a story, prayers and a kiss. If you have had a row say you are sorry and make it up. She may not be able to express sorrow or hurt but by your doing it for her she will feel more secure and gradually become less difficult.

For the older child with persistently bad behaviour, a visit to a child guidance clinic may be well worth the effort. Ask your doctor to give you a letter of referral and to make an appointment for you. It is not an admission of failure to seek expert advice. If you have a toothache you go to a dentist: if your child has a psychological problem then a psychologist may be the person best qualified to help. Explain the position as honestly and clearly as possible so that the clinic has a full picture of the problem. If they wish you and your child to attend the clinic for assessments and counselling over a period of time, then do so. Keep the appointments and do not give up after a week or two. It may be a problem that will take time to sort out; give them that time to help you. You owe it to your child, she deserves the best you can give her.

But do make sure that they tell you what is happening, how the child is progressing, the results of the assessments and their final conclusions. Do not be left, as I was years ago, after months of regularly attending a child guidance clinic about a particular problem, with no information, no results after lengthy assessments, no advice of any sort and a distinct feeling of the blame being placed on me for being a lone parent.

Bed-Wetting

This problem is not exclusive to single-parent families. It can strike the securest of two-parent homes and is as difficult to eradicate there as in the one-parent home. The child may have been dry and then suddenly revert to wetting at night or, less frequently, day and night. There may be no pattern, with several dry nights followed by several wet ones. Cutting down on drinks in the evening and lifting the child at 10 or 11 p.m. will probably have little or no effect.

It is a miserable problem for both sufferer and parent, involving endless rounds of drying clothes, the misery and discomfort of a wet bed, and possibly the added complication of a child or parent who has to share a bed with the sufferer. Then there are the social (or antisocial) consequences: the difficulties of having friends to stay or going to stay with others, going to boarding-school, camping or on holidays, the dreaded rustling and bulk of waterproofing and extra night-wear.

It is extremely difficult to stay calm and offer words of sympathy when you feel like screaming as you face another rainy day with a bath full of sheets and a child who must be sponged down before she can get dressed.

I first read about the device called a **"buzzer"** in a book by an English lone parent and obtained ours through a newspaper advertisement. One type consists of two fine-meshed wire sheets connected by leads to a small box. The box is battery run, has an on/off switch and emits a loud buzzing noise. The metal fabric is placed on the bed, between cotton sheets, and when wet the buzzing alarm goes off, waking the child, who gets up, switches off the alarm and heads for the toilet. Another type is a pocket-sized clip-on battery box which is clipped to the child's pyjama-top with a lead to the child's pants. The principle is to associate the noise with urination and, over a period of time, the mind learns to reorganise the pattern of wetting and sleeping to waking and going to the toilet. Some children sleep on despite the incessant and loud noise of the buzzer, and it is possible to get an extension bell which amplifies the sound.

More in desperation than in hope I rigged ours up (the wire mesh type). It is absolutely safe, with no possibility of electric shock. Within two weeks the pattern was broken and my eight-year-old was either waking and going to the toilet or sleeping through a dry night. After eight weeks I took the buzzer off the bed as it had not shattered our sleep for almost a month. The transformation in the child was amazing; confidence,

132

pride and delight radiated from her. If, for any reason, the bed-wetting should resume, just go back to using the buzzer for a longer period of time to break the pattern.

Buzzers, I have since discovered, are available on loan from your local health board, a fact I have yet to read about in any article on the subject. You need a letter from the clinic doctor or your own doctor recommending one. Do not be surprised if your doctor does not mention their availability; none of the doctors, social workers, psychologists and psychiatrists I approached over the years for an answer to the problem ever did. Specialist medical equipment stores sell them; you could buy one and sell it on later through the Small Ads.

In fact there are mixed reactions to the idea of using the buzzer to cure bed-wetting. Some doctors and psychologists do not approve of this method of dealing with bed-wetting, or enuresis, to give it its medical title. Many professionals will tell you the child will grow out of it and that you should ignore the problem, be cheerful and encourage the child to have confidence. But after eight or nine years of wet beds, and perhaps several children in the family wetting, how cheerful can you be? There are other treatments for bed-wetting, some based on special diets and on drugs, and you could ask your doctor about these also. In any case your doctor may want to rule out kidney or bladder infection or some other medical problem.

Fretting, Weeping and Clinging

Children, just like adults, have different ways of expressing emotion. In the frantic round of single-handed coping, it takes superhuman effort to devote as much time and attention to children as we would like to, given the choice. In an effort to keep all the wheels turning, and our lives in one piece, we almost will our children into growing up faster. Mentally and physically we push them towards some degree of independence in the hope of alleviating some of the burden and the demands on our time. But you cannot rush your children into growing up; they must live through each stage of development at their own pace.

Some months after my marriage broke up, I went with my children to live and work in a children's home. My daughter was barely three years old. For the seven months we were there she alternately resisted everybody and everything, and slept, often on the floor or where she sat. I worked long hours minding up to thirty small children, and my daughter bitterly resented this. When we left the home she spent virtually every moment of the day and night with me for the next six months. I worked as a child-minder in a private house, taking her with me each day. As I worked she spent endless, happy hours playing with water, reportedly a very soothing and calming experience. She has grown into a confident, capable and independent young woman with practical skills and a wonderful way with children.

There is the child who frets every time you go out, or the one who cries and clings to you if you so much as reach for your coat or when you take her to school (this happened with my son after I had been in hospital).

There is no instant cure or remedy. Your child is trying to cope with the terrible fear that you, her sole remaining parent, may disappear out of her life. While she can see you and be with you, she is content, but she

134

cannot cope with even temporary separation. Give this child loads of love, affection, attention, and take her with you whenever you can. Let her come into bed with you, if she wishes, but tell her you will pop her into her own bed later so that you can sleep. If you must go out and leave her, tell her where you are going, with whom and at what time you will return. This way she has a mental picture of where you are when you are not with her and, if need be, you can wake her and tell her when you come home. Gradually she will overcome this fear and develop a sense of security.

I asked my daughter, who is now nineteen, to put on paper her memories of what it was like growing up in a one-parent family. I was shocked to see how frightened she was that she might lose me and be all alone in the world with only her brother. I had been quite ill, in and out of hospital, and because, as she says, she was only a child of six or seven, no one bothered to explain to her that I was sick but would not die.

So try to take the time in the midst of your own worries and problems to reassure your children and explain to them what is happening.

Telling your Child's Teacher

Your child's teacher should be made aware of the home situation for several reasons. Part of building up a relationship with the child is knowing a little of her background. If the teacher unwittingly sends home notes addressed to Mr when there is no Mr, tells all the children to get their fathers to take them to a sports match or to make gifts or cards for a mother they do not see any more, this can cause distress and embarrassment to a child. Also, children can be quite callous and keep asking the one-parented child where her father/mother is and why he/she never comes to the school. If the teacher is aware of the situation he or she can help smooth the way for your child.

As a working lone parent, stress the importance of timely notification of free days, half-holidays, school holidays and parent/teacher meetings. I used to end up in tears of frustration, arriving at the school to be told that there was a free day or half-day that day. This is hopeless, when you yourself have to be at work in half an hour and have no arrangements made for your child/children. A written list of all holidays at the start of each term would be a simple, efficient method of saving the sanity of the working parent (or indeed any parent).

Learning Problems

If your child has a reading, learning or emotional problem, talk to her teacher. In classes of thirty-plus your child's difficulty may go unnoticed or uncorrected. If help is not forthcoming or if you would like an independent assessment, your doctor or local health board will be able to refer you to the appropriate agency. Do not wait, being too shy or polite to approach the teacher with a problem which you feel is in his/her area more than yours. I know many parents whose children's various reading or learning difficulties went undetected for years. The cry was the same in all cases: "If only we'd spoken up earlier, when we had a feeling all was not well, but we thought the school would tell us if anything was wrong." The school may well tell you, in some very obvious cases. But the average teacher who has thirty to forty children to a class, a syllabus to keep to and who may be largely unqualified to spot remedial

136

cases, can easily let the child with the learning problem just drift on, struggling to keep up until she drops hopelessly behind. Besides, lack of remedial back-up in the school may disincline teachers to highlight cases. So get in there and speak up. Your opinion has value and is vitally important to the welfare of your child.

Some Advantages

Your child may exhibit no problems at all. She may be of tremendous help, support and comfort to you while displaying no rancour towards the absent parent. Philosophically, she may accept that, while this new way of life has its shortcomings, it can be fulfilling and harmonious, building great bonds between parent and child. One pleasurable feature of our small family was the absence of distinct parent/child roles. We did a lot of things together, as friends. Because there was no adult partner for me to talk to, I talked to the children about plans, ideas, items of news or topics of interest. We went swimming, visiting, walking or to the library together. There was a practical reason for this: there was only me and if I went, they went too. The spin-offs are worth it too. We have a good relationship with no taboo subjects and a degree of communication which has continued through their teenage years and into adulthood.

Here, in fact, is an area where your child as one of a lone parent may actually gain over the two-parented child. All the loving and giving you would normally share between spouse and child goes straight to the child; all the chatting, sharing of ideas, late-night snacks or hugs in bed on Sunday mornings are now channelled directly to your child or children, who will benefit enormously as a result.

Helping your Child to Independence

Having an independent life of your own is not something which must be postponed until the children have grown up and flown the nest. They will, in fact, benefit from having a well-informed, self-sufficient parent who is not a martyr to them or to the kitchen sink.

As parents we should gear ourselves towards phased redundancy. Our aim should be to make our dependents independent, thus our role as parent diminishes and we become people first and parents second. That day may seem very far off but, like retirement, we should prepare for it now and see it as a positive thing rather than a black hole, a void or a time to be dreaded. It is very tempting to cling to one's children, to make them the be-all and the end-all of one's life. It is particularly tempting to continue to cherish your kids, to guard them and over-compensate for their one-parent tag; after all, they have only you. The wheel may go full circle and you end up having only them, and resent their leaving home or smother them with care in the hope that they will prefer to stay with you rather than seek independence. Do this and you risk one of two reactions: resentment or rejection and a race to get away from you at the first possible opportunity; or alternatively a clinging dependent adult who cannot face the world without you.

According to one wise and experienced lone mother of now adult children, the secret is to learn to let go and let them go, encourage the timid and unadventurous and learn to trust and have faith in the one who stalks out, slamming the door and swearing never to return.

As young people we probably all did something that distressed our parents or caused them worry or pain. For those whose family has the open-door policy, how reassuring to know that you can come home to a welcome, acceptance and an open mind.

Where Independence Begins

Independence is not something we hand to our children when they reach their eighteenth birthday. It begins way back in childhood, and for the lone parent, it is an especially important part of family life. If you are going to work outside the home, look after a family, and run a house, you are not going to be able to do it all without help. Enlist (or conscript) the help of your child/children. Explain that the system will not work without team-work; if everyone helps, then everyone will have more free time and no one will feel exploited.

Teach them how to do certain jobs, like polishing shoes, making beds, laying the table, or cutting the grass, and then do not expect them to do it all right all of the time, because they won't. But if they know how to they may well surprise you with breakfast in bed or a chore done in your absence. Encouragement, praise, showing them how to use the cooker, iron, lawn-mower, and letting them know that they are welcome to join in, all work wonders. As they get older, each can have her own particular job, for instance putting bins out on bin-day, vacuuming, clothes-hanging or whatever needs doing. Everyone pulling his or her own weight becomes vital for the lone parent who is usually doing three jobs at once all the time.

I am convinced that, as studies show, the children of working parents are usually more responsible, capable and independent than their peers with stay-at-home mums. They have learnt how to do things for themselves and how to share the family burdens, all good training for life. But remember: encourage, don't nag. Hard-and-fast rules are made to be broken, so throw the schedule out the window occasionally and let everyone have jam doughnuts for tea in the sitting-room.

Child-Minding Choices

Child-care facilities are one of the first considerations for any lone parent. If you have a baby or young children you cannot go out unless (a) you take the family with you or (b) you arrange substitute care. If you must work outside the home, child-care is going to be essential to your ability to cope. A working lone parent is leading a double life, and the stresses and strains of this will be directly related to the type of provision you can make for child-care. Your working hours and the ages of the children will determine the type of care needed. Availability of family or neighbour support, your income, where you live, and whether or not you have transport, will all also influence your choice.

Day care centres subsidised or funded by local authorities are too few in number and do not relate to the needs of working parents today. For example, there are too few day nurseries, and many local authority day nurseries close for the first two weeks of August. Some of them do not keep hours comparable to office or factory working hours; others close too early to be of use.

Child-minding is not a "once-off" problem, nor is it something we can be casual about. The question of who minds our children, and the effects on them of unsuitable care, must be given the most serious consideration. Most lone parents walk a tightrope, trying to balance holding down a job and caring for children, as the alternative is to stay at home, caring for the children yourself and living at subsistence level, feeling isolated and deprived. Here then are some options open to you.

Local Authority Day Nurseries

In each of the health board regions there are subsidised day nurseries and day care centres. Ask at your local health centre for addresses and details. Some cater only for children from two to five years, but others take babies under two. Their opening hours appear to vary considerably; some are open from 8.30 a.m. to 6 p.m., others work two sessions, one in the morning, one in the afternoon. Charges also vary, but discretion is used and fees can be varied according to circumstances. Single parents get priority in all cases so, even if there is a waiting-list, do enquire or ask your social worker.

Private Nurseries, Crèches

The number of private nurseries is increasing all the time, particularly in large urban areas, reflecting the return to work of more and more mothers. However, the average fee for a five-day week, 8.30 a.m. to 6 p.m., is £40 per child, a not inconsiderable amount for someone on a low wage, which precludes many lone working parents. Standards vary but would appear to have improved, due to competition and the general demand for mental stimulation as well as physical care. Some of the nurseries have built-in Montessori or play schools which the two- to five-year-olds attend as part of the day. Some nurseries provide food, others don't. Some may even be able to collect your child from school and provide after-school care.

The universities and some large companies/organisations (such as RTE) provide work-place crèches, but this type of provision has not yet caught on in Ireland, despite the increasing number of mothers and lone parents working outside the home. The company who masterminded luncheon vouchers in the U.K. now have child-care vouchers. Employers can now offer these vouchers as a staff benefit, and they can be used as payment or part-payment for child-minders, nurseries or nannies. These child-care vouchers are taxed as income to the recipient but are not liable for National Insurance, which saves both the company and the employee money. A similar scheme in Ireland would really recognise the worth of working parents. In the meantime, contact one-parent organisations for likely nursery places, and also see the special notice columns of local newspapers.

Playgroups

Playgroups are exactly what they say, groups of small children (generally three- to five-year-olds) playing together. As most playgroups operate only part-time and generally encourage parental involvement, they are not really suitable for working parents. Fees, opening hours and play facilities vary. Your local health centre, school, or parish may have a list of the playgroups in your area. Some new housing estates have community-run playgroups, organised by the parents and partly funded by local authorities. These can provide great support for new or single parents.

Not all playgroups are registered with the Irish Pre-School Playgroups Association, much as that Association would wish it. Registration would help ensure that all playgroup teachers and play-leaders were trained and that certain minimum standards were adhered to. For information about registered playgroups in your area, contact the Irish Pre-School Playgroups Association (see Appendix One).

Child-Minders

There is no provision for the registration of child-minders and no minimum standards need be observed. Child-minding is a private service and all arrangements, financial and otherwise, are made between parent and minder. Anyone can set up as a child-minder and the conditions and facilities can vary from great to ghastly. If you employ the services of a child-minder, do ask lots of questions and have a look at the place where your child will be during the day, including the kitchen, bathroom and garden. Enquire about sleeping facilities, play space, toys, food, the number of children cared for, and whether the minder has any child-care qualifications or training. It is not that child-minders are bad, many are wonderful mother-substitutes and care for the children as if they were their own. But realise that your child is continually growing and developing and the time spent with a minder is very valuable and vital to her development. Babies and young children need mental stimulation as much as physical care, so ensure that your child-minder provides this. If you are lucky, your child-minder could become a second mother to your child and her family a second or extended family. This network will be invaluable to you as a working parent and a tremendous boost to your child's security and development.

Fostering, Day Fostering

The Eastern Health Board has expanded its service to families by way of day fostering. The scheme may be expanded to other health board regions, so if you live outside the EHB region, keep asking. The service is arranged between you, your social worker, and the foster parents. The difference between fostering and day fostering is that with day fostering the child or children return to their own home each night and at weekends. This keeps the family together, provides continuity and stability for the child, and allows the parent to work. It also allows "breathing-space" for the foster family. The health board pays the foster family an allowance and the parent pays a contribution according to his/her means. If you would like to know more about day fostering contact the Fostering Resource Group (see Appendix One).

Baby-Sitters

Professional baby-sitters or nannies are extremely expensive as they usually operate through an agency, which selects and places the sitter, charging a fee for this service as well as wages for the sitter for the duration. Contact the Golden Pages for agencies.

Any private arrangement with a baby-sitter will be entirely up to you and therefore your sole responsibility.

Choose your sitter carefully, taking into account the ages and number of your children, the number of hours needed and whether you expect help other than actual child-minding (for example, is she expected to cook and clean as well?). If the sitter is a teenager, it is wise to check with her parents that they know and approve of the arrangement; also, you should find out whether she has baby-sitting experience and is therefore suitable to be caring for your child or children. Always leave a telephone number where you can be contacted and, if possible, notify a neighbour that you have a sitter in, as a sort of cross-check on both your children and the sitter. Do the children like the sitter? If not, why not? Be aware that a number of sexual abuse cases have involved teenage male baby-sitters, so if your children voice displeasure at a particular sitter, do listen to them. Having a regular sitter, or even several regulars, is better for your children than different strangers.

Students and voluntary organisations arrange free baby-sitting, at least in Dublin. One-parent family groups such as Cherish and Gingerbread may help out with baby-sitting among their members. Contact them for further information. (See Appendix One for addresses.)

Domestic Help, Housekeeper

Paid domestic help may be expensive and hard to find, depending on location. Getting someone who is conscientious and reliable is difficult but important. However, if you go out to work and can afford it, paid domestic help can be a marvellous way to solve child-care and housekeeping problems. Word of mouth is probably the best way to find a good "daily," although housekeepers who live in are usually found through employment agencies or the Jobs Vacant columns of newspapers. A live-in housekeeper will not come cheap and you also need a spare bedroom and possibly additional enticements like her own TV. For some lone fathers or mothers working long hours whose salaries are high, a housekeeper may be the answer. In any event, consider the additional expenses in hiring a housekeeper—social insurance contributions, meals, light and heat, linen, phone calls. Some people dislike having a "stranger" living in their house.

After – School Care

Ironically, this is probably the most neglected area of child-care, despite the shorter hours needed. There is no organised provision made for the children of working parents from school-finishing time to work-finishing time. Here it is up to the individual parent to make arrangements. For parents who work full-time, this creates stress and worry unless they are in a position to arrange and pay for alternative care. As mentioned earlier, some day nurseries will take in children for after-school care, as will private child-minders. You could pay someone to come into your home or to take the children into theirs. This arrangement could include giving the children an evening meal and supervising homework. A system that worked well for me some years ago was having a woman come to my house each day at 3.00 p.m. to be there when the children came in from school. She would supervise homework, keep them company, clean the house and start the dinner. As I arrived home at 6.00 p.m. she was ready to leave.

Other people find friends or neighbours who either take the children in or come to your house. For some children your working will mean their coming home to an empty house. Working part-time may help solve this problem, but there still remains the problem of school holidays.

School Holiday Care

Depending on the ages of your children, and where you live, you may be able to overcome the long holiday problem by a combination of summer camp, child-minder and your own annual leave. Special holidays for children, including summer camps, are dealt with separately (see Chapter Six). Where possible, take your annual holidays during the children's vacation as, apart from the saving in baby-sitting fees, it will give you and them some time together, even if you cannot afford to go away on holiday.

It is no harm to let it be known that help with school holiday care would be welcome. Family, friends and neighbours can be kind and good about including your kids in their holiday activities, or in just keeping an eye on them for a few hours. The social worker or even your family doctor may have some ideas of likely sources of help, so speak up. Mutual help, where you mind a friend's child one day while she minds yours another day, can often be the solution to both your problems, but it obviously requires that you have some free time.

6

Practical Matters

Holidays

I know, I know! There isn't enough money or time for a
holiday. Think of the cost, and the bother and the fuss.
Where would you go, and anyway, you've never gone on
a holiday without having your parents or your husband
or wife for help and company. Who ever heard of a
holiday on your own with the children, or even without
them?

Why not? Okay, there are the practical problems like
money, time off and where to go, but basically it is
possible to go on holidays. So consider the options.
Perhaps you can go either with, or to, friends or
relatives or on a group holiday such as those organised
by Gingerbread (see Appendix One), who run outings
and holidays for lone parents and their children.
Alternatively, you and the children can set off on a
holiday of your own choice and making.

Some Ideas

Do you know of anyone with a holiday house or caravan
who would lend or let it for a week or weekend? Could
you swap your house or flat with a family from another

part of the country—or even from abroad? Consider renting or borrowing a tent, or offer to mind a house and feed the cat, dog, horse or guinea pig while friends or relatives are on their holidays.

I have done one or other of these things over the years and the children and I had the most wonderful holidays, all at minimal cost. The point is, holidays need not mean hotels, lavish food and entertainment, souvenirs or good clothes. All our holidays were welly-boots and jeans affairs; lots of walking, climbing "mountains," blackberry-picking and playing on the beach (wrapped in three jumpers and an anorak, if necessary). All our entertainment came compliments of Mother Nature—collecting shells or leaves, making dams in streams, talking to horses or cows, etc.; all the fresh air gave us hearty appetites and good complexions and we slept like logs.

An instinctive first reaction to the idea of going on holiday as a lone parent is the lop-sided feeling of it. Friends' and neighbours' reactions will not be much help here. Either you are "very brave" or "a bit odd" going off with just the children. But one-parent families are families too, who work, interact and behave just as two-parent families do. There is nothing brave or odd about going on holidays, whether there be one parent or two present.

Besides, it is a great way of getting really close to your children and this is tremendously important. Most lone parents spend from early morning until late at night rushing about, doing too much and trying to be in too many places at once; helping with homework with one hand and preparing dinner with the other. It is 10 p.m. before you fall into an armchair (or bed) and realise that you hardly had time to speak to your children apart from "Brush your teeth" or "Have you got

149

your school lunch?" Whole days and weeks are going by and the day-to-day problems are gobbling up the precious time when you should be enjoying their childhood with them.

A holiday may give you the breathing-space you need: a change of scene, a break in routine, time to relax, talk, sleep, go for walks, write letters, read. There is time to do what **you** want to do and time to do nothing at all without feeling guilty.

Going on holidays on your own does not mean spending all the time on your own. If you play tennis or cards or swim—invite a fellow-visitor along or ask the next-door neighbour in for coffee. Children are a great way of making friends, as are pets. Chatting to local people is a good way of finding out about places of interest and local entertainment. If transport is a problem ring up Bus Éireann or Irish Rail and ask about off-season, mid-week or special cut-price excursions. Check the newspapers for advertisements of special rates and reductions for children. Make enquiries; perhaps you could pay petrol costs in exchange for a lift with a friend going your way.

Holidays for Children

If funds are not too scarce and the children are of an age and interested, there are lots of summer camps available around the country. These are usually well advertised in the newspapers, particularly local ones, early in the summer. Basically there are three types.

Day Camps

Here the children attend from 9 or 10 a.m. to 1 or 4 p.m. approximately. They are usually run from one to six or eight weeks during the summer recess, each camp lasting a minimum of one week. There are sports-orientated camps, arts and crafts ones, drama and literary-based ones, or ones which combine all three. They are usually based in local schools (though not necessarily organised by the school). Costs of these camps differ, materials are generally supplied though lunches are not, and there are sometimes reductions in fees where two or more children of a family attend or if you pay before a certain date.

Residential Summer Camps

These are similar to day camps but the children reside in the school for the duration. Here meals, accommodation and materials are supplied. These camps are obviously more expensive and fees vary. Perhaps a more affluent parent, in-law, grandparent or relative could be persuaded to help financially in lieu of birthday presents or other gifts.

Community Camps

These are organised by parish communities and voluntary groups or students and are very popular. They are run on similar lines to the day camps mentioned, but fees are usually lower and probably negotiable, depending on your circumstances. Your clergyman or health centre should be able to tell you what is on; otherwise ask at the town hall or library. St Vincent de Paul organise holidays for children; ask your local health visitor or social worker.

Alternatively, friends or relatives might agree to have your child/children to stay for a short holiday, if you, in turn, mind theirs while they go away some other time. Even two-parent families find it extremely difficult to get a holiday without the children. One of the advantages of being an independent lone parent is that you can move into their home and take over the reins with no formalities. Weekends when I minded other people's children in their homes were "mini-holidays" for my own children.

Another option is to advertise your services for week-end or week-long child-minding on a paying basis.

Holidays on your Own

If you can arrange to have your offspring cared for, and you have a few spare pounds, consider the possibilities of a holiday on your own. It is quite fashionable to advertise for company for holidays. There are holidays to suit every age-group and personality. These include adventure and activity holidays, leisure (lazy) and cultural types, pilgrimages and even grape-picking holidays. You can travel by bus, boat, train, plane or bicycle. You can even camp, pony-trek or walk, as in hitch-hiking or hill-walking.

Where to Look for Details

Try travel agents, the columns of newspapers and magazines, clubs and groups associated with holidays or "singles" groups. The National Youth Council of Ireland (see Appendix One) publishes an annual directory of summer activities and opportunities for young people, or try USIT (the Union of Students in Ireland Travel). Phone or write for details.

A word of caution, though. Young children have no concept of time. If you leave them, they cannot understand or realise that you will be back. If they are too young to understand, do think carefully about leaving them. Never leave children with strangers or anyone not very well known, both to you and to them.

Some Ideas for the Good Days

Becoming self-sufficient not only makes practical sense but is also a great psychological boost. There is nothing so satisfying as mending the dripping tap that has plagued you with its constant drip-drip these past three months. There are so many little things that got done by the man of the house (even if in bad grace or sporadically) that are now suddenly your problem. So what do you do? Pay a plumber, carpenter or electrician, if you can find one, supposing you can afford it? Borrow a neighbour or friend? Or have a bash yourself?

By self-sufficiency I mean running a house, garden, car, and doing most of the minor maintenance yourself. You will not be able to do everything yourself and occasional help will have to be enlisted, even if it is only to supply the necessary tools.

But plugs and fuses will blow, the heating will break down, the children's bikes or the pram will need repair, the vacuum-cleaner and/or the lawn-mower will need attention and the drains unblocking, at some time or another. The library and your local bookshop are full of books on self-help house repairs and DIY manuals of various types.

If you do not know where to get parts or how to do a job, ask someone who does. You should learn how to do it yourself and not have to rely on someone else to do it for you. Fine if you can afford to pay or someone offers to help, but you may need to know yourself. Apart from really old clothes, you will need a few basic tools: large and small screwdriver, hammer, set of spanners, some lubricating oil and a vice grip.

If the heating breaks down on Christmas morning, no amount of money will get it mended, but if the fault is minor it may be possible to get it going, even temporarily. If you are blessed with teenage children, then perhaps they will tackle the messier or more mechanical jobs. Teach them how to maintain their own bicycles. Certainly, gardening, decorating and running repairs should be within their grasp, and woodwork or metalwork teachers at school could be consulted. If your living conditions are dreary, even small children can strip wallpaper and have a ball doing it. Mind you, explain clearly which room you want stripped and preferably lock all others!

Tricks and Thoughts on Saving

I absolutely refuse to go into the finer arts of recycling rasher rinds and suchlike as a means of saving money. I am of the opinion that if you are at an all-time low then the thought of tripe or boiled brains is enough to make you call it a day.

Trying to live or exist on a ridiculously low budget is not peculiar to one-parent families. The cost of living and unemployment levels have risen remorselessly, leaving a large chunk of underpaid, underprivileged, low- (or no-) income families, social welfare recipients and old age pensioners trailing further and further behind. For example, there has been a 90 per cent increase in the number of women living on social welfare over the last decade. As a nation, we spend millions of pounds each day on alcohol and horse- and dog-racing, while meat once a week is a luxury not all of us can afford.

The following then are some guidelines and ideas on how to juggle, scrimp and save and get the maximum out of the minimum.

Shopping

What not to do

- Don't go shopping when you are hungry or tired.
- Don't (if possible) go shopping with small children, especially if they are hungry or tired.
- Don't shop at peak shopping times.
- Don't impulse buy. Always ask yourself "Do I really need this?" If the answer is no, then don't buy it.

What to do

- Make a shopping list with quantities, sizes, etc. and stick to it.
- Shop only once a week (if budget allows this). Buy larger sizes, after checking that there is a saving, and "own brand" labels; check quantities on packets and bottles marked "Special Offer."

- Shop around if you have the time or at least compare prices, say from newspaper adverts.
- Never go shopping for just one or two things: always wait until you have a list of jobs to do or items to buy and combine shopping with school collection, church-going, business appointments or whatever.

Buy or borrow a shopping bag with wheels. You may feel a bit daft at first pulling it around (and mind people's ankles!) but it is a wonderful asset. Your hands are left free to examine goods, find your purse, compare sizes, or measure clothes on kids; it saves your arms from aches and your back from possible back strain (carrying heavy loads is very bad for you). You can shop at a much more leisurely pace and take advantage of heavy goods at knock-down prices. It is doubly useful if you live far away from shops, travel by bus or train, have been ill or are frail; and, at Christmas-time, a trolley is just great for loading all the food and presents into as you battle through crowded streets and stores for breathing-space.

Other Savers

Freezers and their Merits

Talking about freezers to single parents is perhaps like recommending that everyone have a Rembrandt painting on their wall or a Rolls in their driveway. Some of you will probably have a freezer already. Those who don't but who may have contemplated buying one will possibly have worked out their advantages versus their cost, money being the deciding factor.

There is no doubt that there are tremendous savings in preparation, cooking time and money in having a freezer. You can buy in bulk in season, prepare a week's meals or bake six cakes and loaves at one time and use the time saved for you, your children or whatever. They are a wonderful asset to anyone working full-time with a family to feed. You can make litres of home-made soup or mince stew on a Sunday night and thereby cope with any unforeseen eventuality during the coming week. But if you would have to go into debt to buy a freezer, then forget it; they are not worth that.

As an alternative, if you have close family or friendly and obliging neighbours with freezers you could, perhaps, have the use of a portion of their freezer, doing something for them in return. As freezers cost less to run when full, it could also cut down on their electricity bills.

"Bake-In"

You might also consider what some people I know do, having a "bake-in." A group comes together for a morning (or evening), pools ingredients and bakes a load of pies, cakes or dinner dishes at one time and freezes the lot (either separately or collectively). Besides stocking up the freezer, it seems a productive way to have some social life!

If you are interested (or merely curious) in investing, talk to a freezer-owner, preferably one with a large family and/or a hectic schedule. Do not attempt to approach a sales representative until you have made up your mind and know exactly what you want.

Buy a Pressure Cooker

Somehow! Even if it means putting some pence away each week to save for it, get one; it is worth it. It saves in time and electricity, it is not difficult to operate and you can prepare hot stew in thirty minutes. If you are out working all day and have all the chores and the dinner to get when you come in, a pressure cooker is invaluable and you will eat better than you otherwise would.

Good-As-New Shops

These have become very popular and quite respectable and acceptable for buying both adults' and children's clothes and sometimes shoes. They seem to cater for everyone, selling anything from sun bonnets to school uniforms. Some go in for designer clothes and evening wear, others specialise in children's clothes, but most carry a bit of everything and buy as well as sell.

Sales of Work/Bring and Buy Sales

These are great places for buying birthday presents or Christmas gifts, home-made cakes and jam, and books for thirty pence or less, as well as second-hand clothes. October to Christmas is the most popular time for these sales.

Auctions

Auctions or the "Articles For Sale" columns in newspapers are the places to look for furniture, baby gear, washing-machines and expensive things like bicycles, train sets or stereos.

Advertising

Stick a notice in your local shop or supermarket and you may get anything from a bicycle to a baby-sitter, prams to piano lessons.

Street Markets

These are good for fruit and vegetables and for all sorts of goodies at Christmas-time. If you buy electrical goods, do get them checked out for safety before use, especially flexes, and replace the plugs with new safety ones.

Second-Hand from Friends

"Passing on" has become a most acceptable and fashionable practice and even the most well-heeled now have swap parties for both adults' and children's clothes. Here, amid much hilarity and coffee-drinking, you can obtain really good, even expensive clothes either as a swap or at a bargain price. Never say no to second-hand clothes from friends, especially for the children. Any that are not suitable can be passed on to other friends or to a charity (who may even call to collect the stuff if you ring them).

People are sometimes shy to offer clothes, fearing that you will be insulted. But getting a bag of clothes can be like Christmas with everyone pulling out stuff saying "Bags I this one" or "Yippee, just the colour I wanted." If some things are slightly bizarre, like the purple lurex shirt we once acquired, well, the "dressing-up box" will be all the richer for it.

Never buy a book that you could borrow or get from the library, unless you need it for study or reference—like this one!. Get people to give you books or book tokens as gifts instead.

Magazines can be passed on and on and on. They have become prohibitively expensive to buy but are a great form of relaxation, and some are full of useful hints and nice recipes, patterns and ideas. For years friends passed on their magazines to me, none the worse for being slightly out of date. I, in turn, gave them to hospitals who seemed no less pleased than I to receive them. Alternatively, give them to the children who can spend wet afternoons making collages and posters from the pictures.

Food for Free

If you know what to look for, the hedgerows and ditches can be a source of food; blackberries and mushrooms are obvious examples. Nettle soup is simply delicious, easy to make and highly nutritious, but only use the tops of young nettles in season and pick well away from roads and industry. Growing your own is another cash saver but is more labour intensive. Both can be rewarding and enjoyable pastimes. There are a number of books on the subject, so try your library.

However, as the vast number of people who most need "food for free" live in towns and cities, with pollution and not so much as a window-box, this may not always be feasible or easy. (A woman I knew grew tomatoes quite successfully tied to the legs of the chairs in the dining-room and, while they were a bit of a bother at meal-times, they provided a diverting topic of conversation). It takes time as well as space to grow your own food and we never seem to have enough time as it is. But if you do have the time and space, try it. Growing food is a most therapeutic and fascinating experience and is educational and creative for children.

Dressmaking and Knitting

Obviously making clothes yourself costs a fraction of the shop prices, and it allows for a sense of individuality and style without blowing the budget. Pattern styles are smart and easy to follow, and can be adapted to suit most sizes and shapes. As an alternative, if you have a dressmaking friend, pay her to make for you and/or your children or return the favour some other way, such as baking or child-minding. Certainly, outfits for Holy Communion, Confirmation, weddings, debs balls, and the like, are much cheaper (and more individualistic) made by a dressmaker rather than bought.

Do-It-Yourself Energy Savers

In these days of price increases, fuel shortages and power cuts, if you have an open fire use it, if at all possible with smokeless fuel. Turn country walks into firewood-collecting sorties. Keep eyes and ears open for friends and neighbours cutting down trees and offer to help cut, stack, carry or store it, in return for some logs and kindling. A lot of household waste can be burnt. Put it on last thing at night if you think it may smell. Avoid burning plastics as they may produce toxic fumes—and always use a fireguard.

Fuel Savers

Insulate where you can; bodies firstly but also doors and windows. For draught-proofing you can buy rolls of adhesive-backed foam strips and apply them yourself.

Insulate your attic and lag the hot-water cylinder: you can do both yourself but wear a mask and gloves to protect yourself against the materials used as they may irritate your skin and mucous membranes. Enquire at your nearest electricity showrooms about possible grants to pay for materials, or about special seasonal offers. Ask about paying for cylinder jackets by instalments on your electricity bills. Use your imagination. I once stitched the old curtains on to the back of the new ones to make great, heavy, thick curtains.

Do all clothes-washing, hair-washing, bathing and major dish-washing at one time, to economise on the hot water. Consider getting a night-rate meter fitted. They are slightly more expensive to install and the rental is dearer than the day meter, but the unit charge is less than half the day rate (2.85 pence as opposed to 7.14 pence for the day rate in 1990). With a night-rate meter and a time clock you could run the washing-machine and/or the dishwasher at a fraction of the day rate as you sleep. A shower uses less hot water than a bath but the latter is better for soaking grimy children; soak their dirty clothes in the water when they get out.

Occasionally, especially if you are feeling low, blow the expense and treat yourself to a luxurious, long soak in the bath followed by either a night out or a good book, a hot drink and an early night.

The Bad Days

Coping with Depression

There are the black and grey days which will predominate in the early days of adjustment to your new way of life. Regrets for what was, what was not, or what might have been, are going to sink you to rock-bottom, leaving you feeling depressed, weepy, unloved, bitter and terribly alone. Those are the days when everyone else looks happy, everyone else's husband is taking the wife and kids for a drive or a day out, and you are alone. No one is ringing you up, taking you out, calling in or seeming to care at all.

There is no point in ignoring the fact that there will be days like this or trying to muddle through. They will not go away on their own. It will take time and a lot of determination to banish them and still, occasionally, they will return, like ghosts, to haunt you.

Everybody has a different remedy. Some people walk; others dig the garden, scrub floors, polish everything in sight, go shopping or turn the radio up full blast. The idea is to browbeat the depression into giving up and going away. Work therapy is definitely preferable to moping about and it gets a few chores done. A good cry and a cup of tea will do you no harm and will get rid of pent-up tensions. Taking to drink or tranquillisers may be tempting at a time like this, but it will cause far more problems than it will cure.

If the depression or weepiness persists you could go to your doctor for a check-up. Do not let him/her fob you off with sedatives. You may be genuinely run-down, anaemic or getting the flu, in which case it may be that a course of iron tablets or a couple of days in bed will do a lot more for you than propping yourself up with drugs. These should be taken only as a temporary stop-gap solution or at a time of extreme crisis, and always under medical supervision.

If your marriage or relationship has just crashed in ruins, or fizzled out at last after months or years of limping along; if your spouse has just died, gone to prison or left, you are going to be suffering from shock. It is a physical as well as an emotional shock and you are going to feel as if you have been hit by a bus. Most people find that either they cannot sleep or they want to sleep all the time; that they either eat all the time or cannot look at food. Even getting dressed will be a chore, while make-up and hair-styles are no longer of any importance. This is a very normal way to react following the terrible upheaval in your life. If you feel like this you are perfectly normal. You will feel fine one day and terrible the next, confident one minute and in despair the next. If things get really bad, like a fear that you cannot go on, ring the Samaritans (see the phone book).

Try to do a little every day; set yourself a target and do your best to achieve it. Children are a great help. For their sakes, if only to feed them and get them to school so that you can go back to bed, the effort must be made, and finding that you can do that may give you the courage to face and cope with today and tomorrow. Try to talk to other people, when shopping, at work, leaving the kids to school or going to church; not about your problems but chit-chat. Speaking to people is therapeutic and breaks the vicious circle of aloneness.

Take the initiative with people who know what has happened but who may be embarrassed about what they should do or say. They will be much more at ease and very happy to talk if you indicate that you want to, and may even offer help. It is only by communicating with other people that you will move outside your problems and get them into perspective.

Keep informed: read newspapers, listen to the radio, try to hear at least one news bulletin each day. It will give you a view of the world outside your own small one and will occupy your thoughts as competition for your own problems. Apart from anything else, by reading the newspapers you will get to know of outings, organisations, helping agencies and sources of information, work and advice which you may require.

Gradually then, you will find your feet and face the world again. Take your time, do not be defeated and depressed by set-backs, and travel forward in hope. My own personal philosophy would run something like this: try not to regret things or look back; do not feel bitter, it will sour the present; live for today and look with hope to tomorrow; trust in God for what you cannot take care of yourself. Happiness is peace of mind and personal achievement, not material advantage.

Staying Healthy

A fear that must haunt the mind of every lone parent is that of becoming ill and not being able to cope. If you, as sole bread-winner/mother/father/chief cook and bottle-washer/maintenance engineer/school chauffeur/nappy-changer, are struck down with flu or a broken leg, just who is going to take over even one or two of these roles?

Various studies in Ireland, in Britain and in the U.S.A. reveal that ill health among lone parents is a common and recurring problem. It can stem from many causes: unemployment, low income, dependence on social welfare, overcrowding, poor nutrition, stress, violence in the home, multiple pregnancies—especially too close together, alcohol or drug dependency, boring, repetitive work or work with dangerous chemicals (such as hairdressing, dry-cleaning, etc.). Granted, these hazards affect people other than lone parents, but lone parents are more likely to have to live with a number of these causes simultaneously, greatly increasing the risks to health.

Ill health can manifest itself in different ways. It can be physical in nature, such as exhaustion, headaches, recurrent infections, bowel disorders or low back pain. Or it can be a combination of physical and mental strain creating stress-related symptoms like weepiness, irritability, anger followed by guilt, as well as the physical symptoms listed above.

The wear and tear on your nerves of working, scrimping with money, rearing children, fighting legal or personal battles with your spouse, living alone and taking full responsibility for all decisions, should not be underestimated. The people who most need the support of others are often those whose families are unsupportive or, for various reasons, unable to assist. Society has become so insular that, while you are silently screaming from every nerve-end for help, support and friendship, you would die quicker than ask for it. The truth is that most of us will put our hands in our pockets to give to the various official charities, but we seldom dream of offering to give the woman across the road a few hours' rest by taking her kids out with our own occasionally.

Common sense decrees that if you must work flat out all day, rushing for buses and to and from schools, carrying shopping, washing and babies, on top of keeping a job and a home, then you must get a good night's sleep. For seven months after I separated I could not sleep for more than three or four hours a night. I was terrified of taking sleeping-pills in case I got "hooked." During that time I moved house four times, got a job, studied for, sat and passed two exams—and rapidly ran myself into the ground.

Try not to take on too much. If your mind is going at full tilt with worries about money, where to live, how to get a job or the children's behaviour, do not go straight to bed. Try sitting down with a magazine or a very light book and a large cup of hot milk, cocoa or herbal tea. Try deep breathing exercises, transcendental meditation, or lying on the carpet with your feet up on a chair listening to some gentle music. Gradually drain your mind of all the clutter by pushing out each thought as it appears until you are breathing slowly and calmly. Then go to bed and, if necessary, repeat the deep breathing. If you take sleeping-pills or tranquillisers, take them only under medical supervision and never accept those of well-meaning friends.

Try to eat regular and adequate meals. This may not be easy if your time and budget are restricted. Poverty and poor nutrition go hand in hand, and it is a known fact that mothers skimp on their own diet in order to feed their men and children. This can be a false economy. Your health is vital to keeping your family going and you cannot compromise on it. If you really are too tired to eat, an egg-flip, adding whatever you fancy and can afford to a beaten egg and hot milk, is a great pick-me-up. In fact, an egg-flip and an hour's rest may be of more benefit when you are feeling low than a meal and a mad dash to the next chore.

If you really want to be and feel well all the time, try increasing the amount of raw fruit and vegetables you eat (buying them in season when they are cheaper and more plentiful) and cutting down your intake of red

167

meat, cooked, refined and processed foods, and tea and coffee. Encourage the children to eat porridge instead of processed cereals (which are much more expensive in any case). A fascinating book on this concept of eating is *Raw Energy* by Leslie and Susannah Kenton (see Appendix Two).

Keeping warm may seem ridiculously obvious but lots of us do not. However, it makes sense, keeps the heating bills down and most chain-stores now stock very pretty thermal underwear, not like the "long johns" our grannies wore which were true passion-killers.

What Happens if you are Ill?

If you must take to your bed for more than three days or you have to go into hospital, is there someone to take over? Some people will have relatives who can either come and stay, take the children to their home or call every day to your home. If the illness is short-term and not serious then kindly neighbours may be able to help with shopping and school runs. But for anything which is more serious, or requires hospitalisation, then more definite plans will have to be made.

In the space of one year I was hospitalised three times, for three weeks, a fortnight and finally for two months. Being ill was not nearly as traumatic as worrying about who would care for the children, aged six and eight at the time. In each instance extremely kind friends took the children into their homes and treated them as their own. On the first two occasions I had pleurisy and pneumonia and only a few hours' warning before being admitted to hospital. So when friends offered I very gratefully accepted, having no alternative. The third time, I knew I had to go in for a

168

minimum of two months and set about exploring child-care facilities in such circumstances.

The child-minding agencies I contacted were very expensive and in any case refused to take on such a long job. Health board "home helps," I was informed, were sometimes available but since they do not stay overnight they were not able to take over completely in such a situation. Finally, my local health clinic offered to place the children in a children's home if they could find one to take them, an offer I refused. In this instance the statutory authorities were sadly lacking in information or assistance of a practical nature and failed to comprehend the urgency of the enquiry. With a sinking feeling I realised that here was another area where there is frequently no help at all available at State or local level for the one-parent family. If all else fails, as in my experience, and you must call on family or friends, you may feel that you are burdening them unduly; paying them, even partially, for the child's/children's keep may be a compromise.

The social workers in hospitals should be able to help you to deal with any problems, worries or queries you may have while there. Make sure that you continue to receive your social welfare entitlements, which may mean replacing your unemployment payment with a disability one while you are ill. Ensure that you get the necessary documents certifying your inability to work. If a social worker does not come to see you in hospital, ask to see one; it is part of the hospital service.

Disability Benefit

If you are in employment, make sure that you obtain a certificate, signed by a doctor, so that you can claim

Disability Benefit. Any delay in requesting the forms and sending them in to the Department of Social Welfare may result in loss of payment, so as soon as you are ill, ask your doctor for a certificate.

If you are a medical card holder or are within the specified income limit, you may be eligible for free hospital treatment and drugs (see "Medical Cards," page 37.) If in doubt, ask the social worker. If you have Voluntary Health Insurance (VHI) your entitlements will be dictated by the number of units you have (see "Private Health Insurance," page 40). The hospital secretary will, on request, give you the relevant forms and answer any queries you may have.

The National Social Service Board (NSSB), which staffs the information centres attached to the health centres and clinics, should be able to answer queries and give information on health, community and social welfare services. If they cannot help you themselves, they should direct you to the relevant service. The voluntary organisations such as AIM Group for Family Law Reform, Cherish, the Widows' and Widowers' Associations or Gingerbread will also deal with queries. (See Appendix One.)

7

Pulling Through

Standing up for your Rights

It always intrigues me that a man who is assertive, forth-right and opinionated is described as having drive, ambition or strength, while a woman with similar traits is invariably unfeminine, tough or pushy. We must develop the confidence in ourselves to ask, demand, take action, query, express and value our own opinions, and generally refuse to be sold short for any reason. Assertiveness is not aggression: it is taking control of and responsibility for your actions rather than blaming someone else or deciding that you are a failure when things go wrong. It is about standing up for one's rights, speaking out at obvious injustice and exploitation and demanding changes in legislation, living and working conditions, pay and opportunity, and attitudes to women's roles and place in society.

This is a healthy and positive progression towards a full and independent life; towards a recognition that women are people in their own right, not merely someone's wife or mother. While being a wife and a mother can be wonderful, worthwhile and satisfying, these are not the only roles for women, but rather aspects of women's lives, which some women will embrace, part-or full-time, but which others will not. The alternatives—such as careers, professions or just the absence of children—should not brand these women pushy, tough or unfeminine. Men do not have to choose between parenthood and their profession; neither should women.

Out on your Own

If you have been living with someone for a long time you develop a certain attachment to that person. This attachment is not entirely dependent on a good relationship; it comes about as a result of living in close contact on a one-to-one basis over a period of time. You adjust and become used to the way that person thinks, responds and behaves. Just like you, that person has set ways of doing things and has idiosyncrasies with which you have learned to live by modifying your behaviour in infinitesimal ways. So when a relationship ends there is a sense of loss and the breaking of a pattern which has become a way of life. It can take time to overcome this sense of loss, even for the partner in a relationship which was prone to violence or full of friction and tensions.

Similarly, many people whose spouses have left them still cling stubbornly to their married status and their illusion of "coupledom," even many years after the break-up. They may have got a Church annulment or a Judicial Separation, perhaps even a divorce, but they still see themselves as married. On one occasion I listened to the tears and grief of a woman whose husband had deserted her eleven years previously and gone to England. Her present desolation was brought about by her having received divorce papers in the post. Her dream had been shattered: he was not coming back to her.

While this is understandable, especially for older women whose husbands may up and off after many years of marriage leaving them totally shattered, it is not realistic to continue to live as a couple if you are now alone. It is, for some, a blind refusal to accept what has happened. For others it is a way of keeping the door open in the hope that he will come back. For those whose husband has gone to live with a much younger woman, it is sometimes a form of revenge: "He is damn well still married to me and I won't let him forget it." Sometimes he does come back and the waiting may be worth it. But many women remain alone, isolating themselves in their bitterness, feeling wronged and hard done by, and making little or no attempt to pick up the pieces and start again.

I know it is not easy to face up to the fact that from today you must face the world on your own, when all your life you took it for granted that you and he would face it together. But you are not alone. There are thousands of women, and men, in similar situations, all picking up the pieces of their lives and starting again. You have friends and families who will help, and there are groups, counsellors and organisations there to help you along and to offer advice, a listening ear, practical assistance and the solidarity of like-minded members.

It may be as simple as saying to yourself, "I'm not Mrs John O'Brien. From now on I'm Catherine O'Brien." This may be the first step in asserting your independence; later you may consider reverting to your maiden name to further that independence. While yesterday you might have bought that newspaper or brand of cereal because he preferred it, today you can choose whichever one suits you.

Do not let people take advantage of you because you are a woman alone. Query the price of what you buy; with repair jobs, ask for an estimate, get a second quote or check with a friend or neighbour to see if it is fair. If you work overtime, make sure that you get paid or time off in lieu. If you need an increase in salary ask for one. Women are notoriously underpaid and exploited, mainly as a result of being non-unionised and in part-time, private or casual employment. "The labourer is worthy of his hire"; if you work hard you deserve to be well paid.

Looking for Change

Those who campaign for change in the role of women in society are not seeking anything untoward or bizarre. They are merely looking for rights that have been seen as male prerogatives, unquestioned and unchallenged until now. It must be realised, and there is employment equality legislation to support it, that women just as much as men need fair wages, equal opportunity, choice, improved facilities in working conditions, and child-care, education and justice before the law. We should not and must not be made to feel guilty for trying to protect our own interests and improve our lot, or for earning our living by working outside the home. The greatest inner conflict imposed on working mothers is that imposed by society's attitude: that mothering and an outside job mean both suffer. This need not be the case, and to label working mothers as selfish or neglectful is unfair and untrue.

If you feel that you are being discriminated against at work or elsewhere consult agencies like the Employment Equality Agency, AIM Group, the National Association of Widows, Cherish or the Federation of

Services for Unmarried Parents and their Children (see Appendix One for addresses) and find out what your rights are. Injustices will not go away on their own; you must speak up on your own behalf and these groups will back you. Remember it is in everyone's interest.

It should be stated that women who are separated and seek their legal rights need not be anti-men or anti-marriage. Most people realise that, while their spouse or their marriage failed to live up to their expectations, this does not blacken all men, women or marriage itself.

Marriage—or What?

For all of us experiencing the end of a marriage or a relationship there is definitely a patch of troubled water, a working-through period. The whole concept of marriage may have a very bad odour and yet the alternative, a vacuum, is frightening. Marriage—or what? The uncharted waste between aloneness and independence has yet to be crossed. Some make it, some do not, but for most it is a painful and problem-fraught journey.

The consequences of separation or desertion are particularly painful in Ireland. We have no divorce to rescue us from the ignominy of no man's land. Thus, asserting your independence becomes a two-pronged problem with, on the one hand, personal, emotional and practical difficulties; on the other, a total absence of status, security, social acceptance or adequate legal safeguards which secure for you or your children property towards which you have contributed and which you may wish to pass on to them.

You may feel terribly odd and unnatural in this new limbo state. You will at times feel inadequate, utterly wretched, useless, even mad, unfit to live. If you do, then you are very much a normal person going through a hellishly rough period of adjustment. After all, not only your circumstances have changed but also your evaluation of yourself, your self-image, and this will take time to sort out. One woman's reaction was: "If I'm not married, what am I?"

Do not be put off, discouraged or downhearted. There are acres of wide-open living space out there, when you get used to the feel of it. Do not be too keen to charge into another emotional entanglement or to prove your attractiveness in a succession of sexual skirmishes. Give yourself time to settle down and sort yourself out, before you find out how you fare in the field, so to speak.

Learning to live alone is a series of stages. At first you may hate and dread being alone; you crave company and fear you will go mad living like this, coming home to an empty house, or not having the key turning in the latch to look forward to in the evening. Indeed many people find their own company the hardest of all to take. One way of coping may be to ask yourself: "What am I afraid of?" You may discover that you have likes and dislikes you were never aware of; that you have views and opinions or the wish to know more about certain issues or subjects that you never had time for. Years of "doing" have absorbed all your energy and time. What about all the books you wanted to read, the music or radio programmes you never had time to listen to, the classes or groups you wanted to join, the hobbies or jobs you never got around to, the friends you meant to write to or visit?

Many people hurry into another live-in relationship. If you are tempted, think out what it is you want from one. Is this just a blind rush for the security and social acceptability of another twosome? Is a partner at any price better than the sheer luxury of suiting yourself? After all, it does not have to be an either/or situation. You can choose your company or opt to be alone. But having a friend or a lover is a very different thing to a live-in partner. A full-time, live-in relationship involves a degree of commitment that needs careful and level-headed decision-making.

If you are on the rebound from a failed marriage, newly bereaved or seeking to regularise your unmarried parental status, try this test. Write down all the reasons why you would want to live with someone and then write down all the reasons why you would prefer to go it alone, even for a while. And remember, I am only talking about the period of time directly following your change in status. Writing it down may seem daft, but doing that means you will have to think about it quite analytically, and analysing your reasons for doing things will (or should) stop you acting impulsively. When you have had time to get used to yourself and your new way of life then you can better begin to look about and spread your wings.

Life After Parenthood

Before, during and after we are parents we are also persons in our own right. For most of us, this aspect of our lives has, on the whole, been relegated to a back seat behind the jobs of parenting, coping, doing, caring and thinking of others. For many, it has been a life lived through the lives of those we have been caring for: our parents, spouse, children—and now suddenly we are free.

This situation may or may not occur overnight. There may be periods of temporary freedom in between the responsibilities. In fact, it may be a very good idea to organise the occasional breathing-space; a day away, a weekend, even longer if you can manage it.

On two occasions when my children were very small and I was overworked and over-worried, I left my aunt in charge at home and took myself off for a "day of recollection" run by priests at a local college. This was not from a surfeit of religious fervour, but because the calm, prayerful, all-adult tenor of the day was balm to my harassed mind and very welcome. You might choose horse-racing, fishing, transcendental meditation or hang-gliding. The important thing is to make it different to your normal daily life and, if you so wish it, a way of meeting other people.

In any event, sooner or later, meeting other people and broadening one's horizons is a must. Being shy or unsure of oneself, lacking money, smart clothes, free time or a baby-sitter—these can all be used as excuses and can be overcome. Face it, no one is going to come in, take you by the hand and whisk you off into a social whirl. People ask you once, twice maybe, and if you decline they will leave you be. Going out alone will take a bit of getting used to. The attitude of others is sometimes the biggest hurdle. "You mean you'd go to a party on your own?" Well, why ever not? How can you meet people if you don't try? Actually, going alone has its advantages. You can leave whenever you like or stay all night.

There are night classes, morning classes for parents of school-going children, voluntary work, meals-on-wheels, parish groups, debating societies, sports clubs, farming and political associations. The range of opportunities is endless but you must motivate yourself, look out, find out, get out.

There is not only life after parenthood but life outside parenthood. For most married people these two states are compatible and interchangeable. Couples share companionship, mutual support, sexual activity and social life. For the newly single life is not so simple. Singleness is often imposed on us and this makes the practical realities of being without a partner harder to accept. As a friend of mine once said, "Some choose celibacy, others have celibacy thrust upon them."

The Constitutional prohibition on divorce has not succeeded in preventing marital breakdown in Ireland. Marriages are breaking down and, in the absence of divorce, people are living together, setting up second homes and starting second, extra-marital families. Over the years there are bound to be serious social, emotional and legal repercussions to these relationships. It is sad that we are not afforded the dignity of being able legally to bury our dead marriages and start life anew. But in the meantime life goes on and we must decide how we wish to live it.

Sex for the Newly Single

In Ireland, sexual activity has been regarded as something that is permissible within marriage for the purposes of procreation. Church and culture have combined to make sex the cardinal sin, almost the only sin, with fire and brimstone awaiting the erring soul. Little regard has been given to the huge physical, psychological and emotional release and fulfilment, the caring and sharing of minds as well as bodies which two people can achieve through a loving sexual relationship.

When a marriage ends or a spouse dies, one may spend months, years adjusting to the loss. But sexual feelings usually live on, dormant or not, and learning to come to terms with them is not always easy. Some will not need or miss close bodily contact; others will. Sexual frustration can often sour into bitterness and resentment. Facing up to the fact that you may need and want some sex in your life is probably a healthier, more positive attitude. What you decide to do about it can only be the result of how comfortable you feel about the idea. You may go on quite happily for several years, unaffected and undisturbed by sexual stirrings. But as the day-to-day problems ease and life becomes more stable, you may feel that a part of your life is missing. Or you may be fortunate enough to meet someone who gives a whole new meaning to your life, a friendship blossoms and a relationship develops that may well include physical intimacy as an expression of shared warmth, affection and love.

So, having overcome the practical problems of how to meet someone new, you now have to face the emotional and moral problems of what to do about coping with a sexual relationship. Because it is an emotive and, particularly in an Irish context, a moral issue, raising large question-marks and areas of uncertainty for those concerned. Thus, what is initially a practical problem becomes a moral one, black versus white, right versus wrong, and approaching your clergyman may not be of much assistance. Clergy, like lay people, can hold widely differing viewpoints and this can be confusing if you are looking for guidance on the matter. However, the clergy, along with the rest of society, are realising that dogmatic judgements are no solution to the immense human problems caused by marital breakdown in a country that prohibits divorce and remarriage. There are many sympathetic and understanding clergy and religious with vast experience and understanding in this area who will not be shocked, judgemental or censorious in their attitude towards you. Marriage counselling services often offer advice and help in these matters; their personnel are qualified and understanding, and you can rely on total confidentiality.

If either the thought or the reality of sexual activity leaves you stricken with remorse or guilt, whether for religious reasons or because of what other people might say or think, then obviously you will want to think carefully about your motives for doing it. Is it, perhaps, to prove to yourself how desirable you are, or to hold on to a man or woman whom you think might otherwise leave you? If so, it is not sex that you need but self-confidence and you will find that outside the bed, not in it. Sleeping around does not make you independent, liberated or avant-garde!

Ideally, sexual activity should be an extension of a relationship based on caring, love and mutual respect. The ideal is not always easy to obtain, but hopping in and out of bed with anyone who is available is no substitute and, besides being a sign of immaturity, is damaging to your mind, your body and your reputation.

Take your time. Get to know yourself and the other person well before you head for the bedroom. How a person behaves generally, how thoughtful, considerate or affectionate he/she is will help you to decide whether you wish to take the relationship further. Getting to know someone well may take time, but it is time well spent, and if that person cares about you he/she will wait. And if he or she tires of waiting and moves on to someone else (or threatens to) you may be sadder but wiser as a result.

If the price of a night out is having sex with someone you do not feel comfortable with, then perhaps it is time to reorganise your social life. If lack of communication was a problem in your marriage, try not to substitute sex for communication with new partners now that you are free to choose them. There is more to life than the big orgasm that many women's magazines go on about. Do not be pressurised into situations not of your choosing. If your teenaged daughter was being pressured into sexual experimentation, your advice would be for her to break with the boy. That advice applies just as much now to you if a similar situation arises. Outside of the structured couples-society we are left with choices and decisions for which we are unprepared, emotionally and morally. It is a subject on which no one is prepared to speak clearly and honestly, where people are quick to point the finger but slow to understand or accept.

How to Put a Little Love in your Life

This brings me on to the practical considerations of how to have a sex-life as a single parent. Given that many single parents have to cope with poor housing, lack of privacy, children, jobs and limited spare time or spare cash, it is perhaps amazing that one can have a sex-life at all. It could well be that the strain of trying to conduct a discreet affair, unbeknownst to one's children, family or neighbours, is more bother than it's worth.

Your children's ages and the proximity of the family or neighbours are probably relevant deciding factors.

That said, it is possible, if you are so inclined, to put a little love in your life. Gone (I think) are the days of the stern hotel proprietress who stood glaring at your ring finger as you signed the register. If you are in doubt as to how to sign, there is nothing untoward in signing only one name, his or yours. If you go to a Bed and Breakfast place, you do not have to sign in at all, merely pay on the way out (and the breakfasts are superb, at a fraction of hotel prices). Getting away from it all precludes the possibility of small visitors at midnight or dawn and unscheduled telephone calls or callers. If what was once taken for granted during your marriage now becomes a treat for rare occasions it is only fair to plan it so that you may relax and enjoy it. Life is a struggle often enough.

For many people sporadic, selective sexual activity is probably the usual solution. Sporadic could be once a week, once a month or once a year, and here selective is the operative word. Obviously, if you socialise in mixed company you may have offers occasionally or you may meet someone with whom you would like to go to bed. While being swept off your feet in a moment of passion is romantic and pleasant to fantasise about, there are three rather vital things to consider beforehand and not afterwards: contraception, AIDS and venereal disease.

If ever there was a time when being responsible for one's actions was necessary, this is it. Whatever form of contraception you prefer, natural or artificial, use it. This is no time to be vague, careless or reckless. Don't leave it up to the man, or expect him to take responsibility; he has no responsibility for you, this is

183

your decision. A visit to a family planning clinic, your doctor or the chemist will save you a lot of worry later on. Otherwise, if in doubt, don't do it.

Venereal disease and now AIDS are a risk every time you have casual sex with different partners. You cannot afford just to close your eyes to the dangers and say, "It couldn't happen to me." It could. Make sure it does not by being selective and using condoms; if you have any reason to suspect you may have been infected, go immediately to your doctor or one of the VD clinics attached to most large hospitals.

I suppose we have all been taught, told and warned that doing pleasurable things to ourselves would lead to blindness, madness and sterility. If such is the case is it not amazing that a vast majority of the population is not sightless, childless or in institutions? If having a sex-life is out of the question, if prayer, penance and jogging are not enough and if the need for sexual release haunts your sleepless nights, masturbation is a harmless, useful and consoling (if lonely) way of relieving built-up tensions. If the physical or moral aspects of it worry you, a chat with a sympathetic doctor or clergyman may put your mind at rest. It is certainly better than risking pregnancy or AIDS as a result of casual sex.

Understandably, some of these suggestions may upset or displease some readers. But it is also possible that many readers will have been faced with difficulties relating to the whole question of sex in their adjusted life-styles and be relieved to realise that they are not alone with their problems or worries, nor are they unnatural in any way. Deprivation comes in many forms.

184

There are other considerations besides the practical. A series of casual partners, while boosting your ego, may have serious disturbing effects on your child/children, who may either become very attached to one particular man or woman or resent all of them for taking your attention and/or their missing parent's place. Also teenagers may not wish to be reminded of their parents' sexuality. One friend reports the truculent and boorish behaviour of her grown son when her man-friend calls to take her out. How your children react will very much depend on how you handle the situation. Making an issue out of introducing your new friend to your children will, almost automatically, put everyone on their best/worst behaviour and the resulting strain could make the occasion a disaster. If you treat the matter casually, letting your friend call to the house, join you on outings, share a meal and join in the general chat, then he/she will become accepted as a family friend and not as a rival or a threat.

Cohabiting and Social Welfare

The Department of Social Welfare define cohabiting as "living as man and wife under one roof." If you are in receipt of any social welfare payments, and it is subsequently discovered that you have been cohabiting during the period covering the payment, you will be considered to have been overpaid and must refund this money to the Department. The fact that you are not financially supported is not a consideration.

8

Fathers Alone

Lone fathers face enormous problems, but interestingly, most of the problems are similar to those with which lone mothers have to cope.

Gingerbread Ireland estimate that 20 per cent of one-parent families are headed by men.

Most fathers are left, the mother having died or deserted, giving them little or no choice in the role of single-parenting. Widowers whose wives were ill, or deserted husbands whose wives are alcoholic or play truant, are probably better equipped to take over the family, as months or years of caring for the children and running the home will have prepared them for the final take-over.

But for most men, single-parenting is a daunting task. Suddenly you not only have to bring home the bacon, but cook it and clean up after it as well. Your role as father takes a new twist and you are now mother too. How do you keep on the job, mind the kids, do shopping and housework; all in one day, every day from now on? What gets priority, the children or the job? You need the money but the children need you. How sympathetic or understanding is your boss if you take time off for their

186

measles, dentist appointments or to buy school shoes or books?

Surveys on lone fathers in Britain and the U.S.A. show that many fathers suffer a drop in earnings because of changes of job, lose over-time pay, are unable to work shifts or weekends, and lose out on promotional opportunity due to family commitments. Some of the fathers I spoke to felt that the children had suffered so much upset that being a full-time father was more important than having a wage coming into the house. But they then felt terribly isolated, which depressed them and their self-image suffered. They were conscious also of the ambiguous attitude of those who consider that it is proper for mothers left on their own to give up work and remain at home, but that fathers in the same situation should continue working. There were instances too where fathers, having given up jobs to mind their children, found that being unemployed went against them in custody disputes. As a father seeking custody you must have a job, which is not the case for mothers.

Be prepared for a degree of suspicion and curiosity as to how you came to have the children in your care. More than a hint here of: if a man walks out he must have been a rotten no-good, but if a woman walks out, there must have been a reason. The best solution? Ignore the gossipers and the gossip.

Motherlessness is expensive. Due to inexperience and lack of time, men often choose to buy expensive, convenience foods at nearby shops. Buying clothes, especially for girls, appears to be a big problem; judging sizes and quality of fabrics is difficult for men unused to such things. Having one less adult to feed is no real saving, yet lone fathers lose their spouse tax-free allowance, thus coming into the tax net sooner than before, when they can least afford it. Be sure to apply immediately for the single-parent family allowance.

Many will be cooking for the first time, having to discover what to buy and then how to prepare it. Keep meals simple to start with. Write out a list of menus you can make and rotate them, shopping as necessary. Either buy a simple cookery book or ask friends or relatives for easy-to-prepare recipes. Check the washing instructions on clothes and household items before you buy them, and bring the children with you when buying their clothes. Buy fitted polyester sheets—they save time when bed-making—and never iron anything that is not absolutely essential. Your children will adapt far quicker than you will to the new routine, so enlist their help and encourage them to do things for themselves.

Many men find it difficult to talk about and find help for their problems. You may also find it very difficult to identify with other men because you are doing what is considered women's work, and with women because you are a man. Not being free to socialise with your friends means that you become even more cut off. It is here that lone parent groups like Gingerbread are of great assistance and support. As with women, loneliness seems to be the big problem as well as self-doubt, feelings of inadequacy, desperation, depression, anger and apathy.

Do not make elaborate plans and schedules because they will not work. Initially plan each day, no more, until you get the hang of it. Do not panic or fuss. So what, if you burn the dinner or the kids have odd socks? If family, friends or neighbours offer assistance, accept graciously. If they don't, do not feel rejected. Many people fear to rush in lest they get landed with a job for life. Oddly enough, if you appear to be coping quite well people may be more inclined to offer their services.

Child-care is going to be a major problem for fathers with full-time jobs; but at least if you have a job you are in a better position to afford the necessary care. (See "Child-minding Choices," page 140.) There is an interesting "double-think" attitude where a woman in receipt of social welfare payments needs to be most careful about allowing a man into her home for fear of losing her benefit, yet it is quite acceptable for a man in a similar situation to bring in a woman, as a housekeeper.

In general, men seem quite happy to set up home with another woman, being less concerned about the legal, religious or social consequences of such an arrangement. This, at least, solves some of the practical and emotional problems—for them if not for their children. These men seem more confident, relaxed and, of course, it usually means that they can continue working, resulting in more money coming into the home.

Some of the fathers I spoke with worried how they would cope with daughters growing up. Many felt that there is an affinity between mother and daughter that a father cannot properly replace. Here a female relative or friend might help, or you could approach your daughter's teacher or the mother of one of her friends and explain your problem.

One big plus which the lone fathers I meet all speak of is how close they have become to their children and how much pleasure they get out of watching them grow and develop. For most of them this is an unexpected and

189

welcome surprise and an aspect of parenting they had not previously considered. It is alright for you to enthuse about your child's progress or latest achievement—women talk about their children, why shouldn't men? A lone father sees his children's development at a much more intimate level than many fathers, and the wonder of a growing child is a whole new world. Enjoy it.

9

Matters of Life and Death

Making a Will

With a fatalistic sense of doing the right thing I queued for ten minutes in a stationer's during Christmas week years ago to purchase a printed will form. It then lay untouched for almost four months before I could face the prospect of reading it and filling it in. Only the thought of the ensuing legal mess should I die without completing it spurred me into action.

What is it that makes us shy away from this simple yet vital step to secure our children's future financial welfare?

To quote the printed slip which accompanies the will form, **Hints on Making a Will:**

1. Every man or woman who has attained the age of eighteen years can and should make a will. Failure to do so may cause difficulty, hardship and extra expense to your family and intended beneficiaries.

191

2. Your will must be expressed in plain language. If you are in any doubt as to how your wishes should be set out, do not use the printed will form. Instead discuss your problems with your solicitor. He or she will advise you on how to express exactly what you wish to do with your property.

3. Under the Succession Act if a testator (the person making the will) leaves no children, the spouse has a legal right to one-half of the estate. If the testator leaves a spouse and children, the spouse has a legal right to one-third of the estate. Children do not have an actual right to a specific portion of a testator's estate. They can apply to the court seeking a ruling that provision should have been made for them, if they are unhappy with the contents of the will as it applies to them. Where there is no will, with no surviving spouse, all the estate is divided between the children. This legal right has priority over all devises, bequests and shares on the testacy. However, these provisions of the Succession Act do not cover all eventualities, and it is very advisable that you should make a will.

4. A will may be revoked at any time by destroying it or by making another will.

If a person dies intestate (without making a will) and leaves a spouse and no children, the spouse is entitled to the whole estate. If that person leaves a spouse and children, the spouse is entitled to two-thirds of the estate and the remainder is distributed among the children. If that person leaves only children, the estate is distributed among them.

Other Points Worth Noting

You must name at least one executor or executrix (female) who will oversee the terms of the will and arrange that the beneficiaries get the money, property, gifts or whatever, as laid down in the will.

The will must be witnessed by two people who are not beneficiaries under the will. A spouse should not witness a will, since this would make void any bequest to that spouse. It is also advisable not to have someone who is either too young or too old to act as witness; this is not a legal requirement but a practical one. The witnesses do not need to read the will, but must together witness you signing it and then sign it themselves in each other's presence, with full names, addresses and occupations.

Where wills are concerned, the Succession Act applies only to married families; see wills for unmarried families on page 202 ff. Will forms are only suitable for very simple situations. It is preferable to go to a solicitor, especially in a marriage breakdown situation where the domestic and legal situations are always complex.

It will probably be necessary for you to change your will from time to time as the years go by. A change in your circumstances or those of your dependents (such as one of you being left some money or property by a relation) or your children becoming adults may make it advisable for you to change the terms of your will. The new will will cancel out the old one, which should then be destroyed.

Finally, put your will in a safe place, preferably telling at least one person where it is. It can be deposited with a bank or solicitor.

Succession of Children

Until the Status of Children Act, 1987 became law on 14 June, 1988, children born within marriage had far greater rights to inherit from their parents than those born outside marriage. Children born outside marriage had limited rights to their mother's estate and none at all to their father's when there was no will. When there was a will, children had not and still do not have any absolute (totally unconditional) entitlement. While children born within marriage had a right to ask the court for provision to be made for them in certain circumstances, children born outside marriage had no such right.

Wills

For wills or similar documents drawn up after 14 June, 1988, any references to children or issue or other family relationship include children born outside marriage unless the contrary is expressly stated. The earlier legislation applies to wills drawn up before 14 June, 1988.

This means that if you made a will before that date leaving money or property to your children, then only your children born within marriage will inherit; if you made a will after 14 June, 1988 saying the same thing then all your children are entitled to inherit. You can, of course, specifically exclude some of your children if you wish; you can also change your will at any time.

There is a provision in the Act whereby a child who feels that he/she has not been adequately provided for may, at any age, apply to the court. The court must decide if the parent has "failed in his moral duty to make proper provision for the child in accordance with his means." This provision used to be available only to children born within marriage but is now available to all children whose parent has died since the Act came into effect. Such a child can now apply to the court under this provision regardless of when the will was drawn up.

Where there is no Will

Children born outside marriage now have the same rights as other children to each parent's estate if there is no will. They also have the same rights as other children to the estates of more distant relatives.

Appointing a Testamentary Guardian

In a one-parent family the question of who takes responsibility for the children should you die prematurely is a particularly important one. To safeguard their future welfare, and to put your mind at ease, you can appoint a testamentary guardian, including it as a clause in your will.

This guardian can be a relative, a friend or any person who will accept responsibility for the children and be genuinely concerned for their welfare. Bear in mind that they will be responsible for handling money left to your children and for making important decisions affecting them, so choose carefully. You should, of course, notify the person whom you select as guardian.

Where you are separated or deserted and appoint a guardian by will, your spouse must abide by the terms of the will and become joint guardian with the appointed guardian. The appointed person does not necessarily have to be the person with day-to-day care of the children. A solicitor, school principal, or any person of your choosing could be the legal guardian, with the children living with and being cared for by a relative or friend. The guardian's duties automatically terminate when a child reaches eighteen years of age or upon the death of that child.

Life Insurance/Assurance

No matter what your personal or financial circumstances, some sort of life assurance really is essential. There are many different types of policies, but the ones relevant to the one-parent family are those geared towards safeguarding the family and minimising the risk of the children suffering in the event of your death. The types of options, policies and premiums vary, so do shop around and seek advice from a reliable broker.

A Family Income Benefit Policy

This is probably one of the cheapest policies available. You take out a policy for a set period of years, usually twenty to twenty-five years, normally related to the time when you expect your youngest child to be fully educated and able to fend for herself. Should you die within the period selected, the insurance company will pay an annual sum to your children for the remainder of the period. The amount of the income benefit will be related to the premiums which you can afford to pay. As a guideline, it could be based on your present income, so that, if this is £8,000 or £18,000 per annum, then that is the sum which will be paid out annually if you die. If you take out the policy for twenty-five years and die after ten, then the money will be paid out for the remaining fifteen years of the period. If you survive to the end of the period, then no payment will be made: death was the eventuality you were covering and this has not come to pass.

An Endowment Policy

This is a slightly different form of assurance. You select any period from ten years upwards, taking into account your age and the ages of your children. (The Revenue authorities will grant tax relief only on policies for periods in excess of ten years.) The policy covers your life for a basic sum assured for the set period. So, if you die, your children will receive the agreed sum. But, if after paying your premium each year, you live to the end of the period, then you receive the lump sum.

Generally speaking, policies which pay out a sum at the end of the term in addition to the cover provided are more expensive than those which do not.

Trust Funds and Trustees

If you are concerned about who will actually handle this money in the event of your death, you should appoint trustees who will administer it in the way best suited to your children's needs, such as a living allowance, school or college fees, medical and holiday expenses or whatever. The trustees' names, addresses and occupations will appear on the policy and, apart from notifying them of your intention to nominate them, there are no formalities. A bank will act as a trustee, as will a solicitor or doctor. Any person who is competent and genuinely concerned about the children's welfare may be a trustee, but for practical reasons do not choose someone who is already advanced in years.

The whole area of insurance can be confusing, so before you commit yourself to a certain policy, go along to a reputable insurance broker and get him/her to explain the different policies, clearly outlining your circumstances, the type of cover you need, and your means. The insurance company will probably request a medical check-up, either arranging an appointment for you with a doctor of their choice, or asking you to arrange one with your own doctor.

The Insurance Information Service (see Appendix One) provides impartial information and advice on all aspects of insurance. (See also "Householder Insurance," page 73

10

Stepfamilies

A stepfamily is one which is formed as a result of the joining (within or outside marriage) of two partners, one or both of whom has brought children from a previous relationship to the present family. Many stepfamilies are created as a result of separation or divorce, but many are also formed after the death of a partner. Stepfamilies can take a variety of forms, including those who are stepfamilies only at weekends or during holidays. Stepfamilies present many challenges but a successful stepfamily can bring rich rewards.

It is now seventeen years since I left behind the shreds of my broken marriage and began life as a lone parent. Seven years ago I decided to live with the man I was seeing at the time and who is now my partner and the father of my third child. Having lived alone with my two children for ten years, the decision to set up home with someone was a major one, arrived at after much thought and discussion. My hesitation was not related to any indecision as to how I felt about my partner. He and I were—and still are—very much in love. Learning to live alone had been for me a hard-won experience. Financial and domestic independence had not been easily achieved and I was by then very much used to being solely in charge, and unused to the give and take, compromise and negotiation, that is necessary in all shared relationships. He, in turn, bore the scars of the break-up of his own marriage and was excited but terrified at the idea of a new woman in his life. We discovered that second relationships are very exhilarating on a personal level but very volatile and complex on an inter-personal basis. Your children and your relatives may not be as delighted as you about the new situation!

There are wonderful, satisfying and rewarding advantages in setting up home with someone you love after years of being a lone parent. However, it is a legal, social and emotional mine-field, and it is important that you give serious consideration to the effects and consequences of what you are doing.

The Constitution protects the rights of married families only. Any family relationships that you create outside marriage will have neither legal recognition nor protection. The problems are manifold and manifest themselves in many ways. It begins with what to call the new partner in your life. Boy-friend or girl-friend sounds silly and does not accurately describe the relationship; partner has business connotations, which can confuse people. Socially it is ambiguous enough. Legally it is uncharted territory.

Bearing in mind that you are now entering a legal no man's land, it is advisable to plan, insofar as is possible, to protect yourself and your partner from any legal repercussions arising from either of your marriages. You should also take steps to protect your new family.

Money and Property

■ Tie up as many loose ends as possible from your marriage. Waive your succession rights either as part of a separation agreement or in a Judicial Separation.

■ Draw up a written contract between your partner and yourself, preferably with legal advice. This document can be a civil contract which legally binds the parties and should protect the interests of both. The most important areas are money and property, including succession.

This sounds like a terribly unromantic and mistrustful thing to do, but it is extremely sensible in your new and non-legal relationship. It will protect your interests, give you some limited rights, and take account of the rights of your children and property. In fact, it is now recommended that married couples draw up similar marriage contracts for the same practical reasons. This contract will be the basis for discussion if your new relationship breaks down or if a former spouse tries to contest a will or separation agreement later.

I feel strongly that women should retain or secure financial independence from their men. Do not combine your finances with those of your partner. Plan a budget together, based on your combined resources, then decide on how income and expenditure should be allocated. This can be adjusted and updated from time to time. If one partner brings a lump sum or property to the relationship, you both need to decide how it should be used; should it be shared or should its owner retain it? If you are financially dependent on your partner, it is important for both of you to understand and discuss this situation, accepting its implications for the present and for the future.

As you are not married to your partner, you are not entitled to maintenance or, in the future, to a widow's or widower's pension for yourself. If your partner already has a spouse, then that spouse may be eligible for maintenance or the spouse pension. You or your partner may already be paying maintenance to a spouse. How much does that leave for the two of you to live on? Does this create hardship or antagonism in the new relationship? The best solution is for you and your partner to retain at least some financial independence. This will mean that each of you has some means of income, from employment, private means (such as rent) or possibly some pension. If you are receiving maintenance or social welfare, this payment may cease if you are cohabiting.

With private pension funds problems often arise as to who is entitled to benefit. Unless clear written instructions have been made and the pension-holder names the beneficiary, the pension trust may decide in favour of the first spouse, even where a foreign divorce is involved, unless that divorce is legally recognised. If you, as a wife or husband, die intestate (without making a will), your spouse has a right to inherit. Only by making a will can you make it clear that you wish your partner, not your spouse, to inherit.

It is possible and advisable for you and your partner to draw up very explicit wills and have them checked by a solicitor. Your spouse could contest the will but he/she would not have an automatic right of inheritance. This will enable you to provide for your partner in the event of your death.

If you live in your partner's home, then as a non-spouse he/she does not need your consent to sell that home; it is not a family home under the Family Home Protection Act, 1976. However, if you can prove that you have contributed financially, either directly or indirectly, to its purchase or maintenance, you can apply to the court for an interest in it. Your partner could evict you if he/she so wished as, not being a spouse, you have no legal right to reside there.

If you jointly buy a house, it is important to stress again that this is not a family home under the Family Home Protection Act. Each party owns the house jointly and is entitled to half of the proceeds on sale. The house does not form part of the estate for inheritance purposes and the survivor becomes sole owner. The house contents belong to whoever owns them.

From the experience of several second relationships known to me, I would strongly recommend that you jointly rent a house for a minimum period of one year before you commit yourselves to buying a home together. Split the rent and the outgoings fairly between you, preferably equally, and review the situation at the end of that year. Renting a "neutral" house will put you on an equal footing, neither one beholden to the other. You can experience the dream of living together before you take on a new financial commitment. If it does not work out, you can retreat with minimal legal or financial difficulties.

Violence

Violence in non-marital relationships is not covered by the Barring Order remedies of the Family Law (Protection of Spouses and Children) Act, 1981. If it is a problem, you can apply to the court to take out an injunction forbidding that person from using violence against you. If your partner is being violent to your children or to his own children, you can take out an injunction against him under the Guardianship of Infants Act, 1964.

Children

Guardianship, Custody and Maintenance of Children

The Status of Children Act, 1987 has removed some of the major inequalities which used to exist between marital and non-marital (formerly illegitimate) children. If you have a child by a man who is not your husband, it is possible for that man to apply to become a joint guardian in the same way as any unmarried father. (See "How the Father can Apply to Become a Joint Guardian," page 103) The courts must now recognise all the children a man has when his maintenance to his wife is being assessed, and this includes his responsibilities to the children of any other relationship. If your partner will not maintain his child, you can take him to court under the above Act for child support.

If you set up home with someone and you have children living with you from a former marriage, who gets custody of your children if you die? Your partner has no legal right to custody. This can create pain and confusion at a very difficult time, with former spouses possibly removing a child from the only secure home she has ever known. A carefully worded will can at least make provision for any property or material effects which you may wish to leave to your partner's children or he to yours.

Succession

Under the Status of Children Act, 1987, children of a non-marital relationship have an equal right to inherit from their father's estate as the children of married parents if there is no will. They can contest a will which discriminates against them. It is advisable for you to draw up an explicit will making provision for all your children, preferably by name, especially if you or your partner have children from a marriage.

Living with Other People's Children

Above I have touched on the legal aspects of non-marital families or stepfamilies. On a more practical level, what is it like to take on your partner's past and his/her children in a live-in relationship? Obviously, this is a very personal experience. How people react depends very much on their experiences in their former marriage, their own personalities, and the ages of the children. Complex family dynamics are involved. This is clearly one of the most difficult areas in a second relationship.

Please be aware that just because someone loves you and wants to live with you, this does not necessarily mean that he/she loves your children and wants to live with them. This works both ways; your partner may be very fond of your children, or you of his, but children have very definite views of their own and it is no easy task assimilating the different personalities into a new functioning family unit.

The children of broken marriages and those whose other parent has died have been through an extremely traumatic time. They may still be suffering deeply from the loss of the absent parent or they may have become very used to having just one parent and bitterly resent the intrusion of a new partner who will take away some of the time and attention they are used to receiving.

It is not uncommon for teenagers to reject totally the views, values and ideology of their parents. It is also quite common for fathers and sons or mothers and daughters to disagree violently. If this happens in your family and you are a lone parent, do not necessarily blame your single parent status. It happens all the time in all sorts of families. Likewise, it may happen in your new relationship. Your son may resent and reject your new partner and your daughter may resent the time it takes from her relationship with you. Take time to talk, be honest and be patient. There are no magic cures, no instant remedies or solutions. Each person is expressing his and her own needs and these are bound to conflict and cause friction from time to time. It is quite likely that relationships cannot be cordial while you all live together. If your efforts to make the incompatible compatible only make things worse, try to remove the tension as far as possible rather than pushing people together.

Living with your Past

You and your partner have needs and scars too if either of you come from a former marriage. Insecurity, jealousy, a poor self-image, sexual or emotional hang-ups, fear of rejection or attachment, not to mention financial worries—everyone comes to a new relationship clutching at least some of these. With children to care for, you won't even get a honeymoon to iron out some of the problems before "real life" begins. The ability to communicate openly and honestly is even more important the second time around.

Many of you will still have communications of some sort with spouses to whom you are still married, unless you have a recognised foreign divorce. This may mean ongoing court cases, mediation over maintenance, custody or access, or disputes over property such as the sale of the family home. It may also mean for some that part of your salary must go to support another home and family, perhaps leaving you with very little to maintain your new family. With no divorce in Ireland, there are hundreds if not thousands of new relationships where one or both parties are still tied in some way to a spouse. This creates strain and pressure and requires very careful handling in order to protect all those concerned.

Children in these relationships cannot be unaffected. How they cope depends on how each of their parents is coping and how amicable or otherwise the break-up was. You can best help them by not asking them to take sides, not criticising the other parent (or at least not in their presence), encouraging them to see and visit their other parent, and taking an interest in what they are doing. This applies equally whether you are their parent or the partner of their parent.

If all or a lot of the above stresses the negative, it is because I am trying to pin-point the possible problem areas. There are lots of wonderful, warm and joyous aspects to finding happiness the second time around. Being aware of the pitfalls may help you to avoid at least some of them.

Stepfamily, the National Stepfamily Association in Britain, produces a useful range of leaflets, dealing with teenagers growing up in a stepfamily, grandparents and step-grandparents, having a baby in a new relationship, and other topics. They also offer a counselling service. (See Appendix One.)

Conclusion

In the course of researching for this updated edition, I visited AIM Group for Family Law Reform and studied the case histories of the many callers to their advice centre.

One thing struck me sadly and forcibly—the similarity of the problems being presented now with those of twelve years ago when I worked at AIM as a voluntary helper. Violence, drinking, adultery, lack of communication and the refusal to support or support adequately are still the same problem issues they were in the 1970s. The position of a lot of married women appears to have stuck in a groove—a dependent groove—with husbands wielding the power that money brings and the wife being totally subject to that power. It seems that a "good marriage" is still heavily dependent on the husband's ability and willingness to support his family and on his good and civilised behaviour. If that support and good behaviour is not forthcoming, or is withdrawn, then wives and children become the trapped victims and suffer accordingly.

To my mind there is only one solution to this cycle of dependency on which most marriages either rise or fall. It is that women should remain or become financially independent of their husbands or their partners. Money equals power, and it is apparent that many of the problems of a bad marriage arise from the power that the husband has over his financially dependent and therefore powerless wife.

How women combine financial independence with childbearing is a thorny question. But more and more wives are continuing in or returning to the work-force and successfully combining employment and motherhood. Certain contributory factors are: smaller families as a result of education and contraception, a greater sharing of domestic chores and the removal of the marriage and baby bars in employment. Financial independence will not guarantee a happy or successful marriage. But at least it puts women on a more equal footing with men and, should the marriage not survive, the woman will have work skills and the ability to support herself and, if necessary, her children.

People are living longer than they did in our great-grandparents' or grandparents' time, with the result that marriages last a great deal longer than they used to. This fact, along with fewer children, means that wives have a lot more time free of pregnancy and child-minding and, with automation, fewer domestic chores. We must educate our young people to adjust to these changes which are now radically altering the whole structure of marriage. These are positive changes, but they must be supported by programmes and training in schools for education for life, for career guidance, for home management, for relationships and for parenthood. There is also an obvious need for a radical overhaul of social welfare and family law legislation, and for personal tax relief on rented accommodation and child-care payments. Discrimination against women in employment, in promotion, in appointments to State-sponsored bodies, in social and sports clubs, all need to be highlighted for what they are and eliminated. Until men and women are seen to have equality by right, they will not be treated equally.

Coping alone should not be seen as a negative thing. It is a positive skill that many men and women have to

employ for many reasons. Coping alone successfully
should be the aim, and it is possible to achieve that aim.
I hope that this book will help.

As I started with a poem I would like to end with one.
This one is translated from Sanskrit:

TODAY

Look to this day,
For it is life,
The very life of life.
In its brief course lie all
The realities and truths of existence:
The joy of growth,
The splendour of action,
The glory of power.
For yesterday is but a memory
And tomorrow only a vision.
But today well lived
Makes every yesterday a memory of happiness
And every tomorrow a vision of hope.
Look well, therefore, to this day.

Appendix 1

Organisations for Further Help and Information

Support, Family and Marriage Advisory

Adam and Eve Counselling Service, 4 Merchant's Quay, Dublin 8 (01-711245/711910). Hours (daily): 9.30 a.m. to 5.30 p.m. Assists people with personal/marital and/or family problems.

Adapt, Adapt House, Rosbrien, Limerick (061-42354). Helps lone parents, offers legal and practical advice and provides a residential centre for abused women and children.

AIM Group for Family Law Reform, Help Centre, 64 Lower Mount Street, Dublin 2 (01-616478). Hours (weekdays): 10 a.m. to 12 noon. Provides legal advice, referral and support for people with marital problems. Branch in Community Centre, Dundalk. Campaigns for family law reform; publishes leaflets on violence, family law, judicial separation, maintenance, foreign divorce, and other issues.

Al-Anon Family Group, 19 Fleet Street, Dublin 2 (01-774195). Information centre (weekdays): 10.30 a.m. to 2.30 p.m. Provides help and information for the families of alcoholics. For local branches and centres of youth groups for teenagers see **Alcoholics** in the telephone directories.

Ally, Dominican Priory, Dorset Street, Dublin 1 (01-732200). Counselling and placement for single mothers.

Bereavement Counselling Service, P.O. Box 1508, Dublin 8. Counselling Centre: St Anne's Church, Dawson Street, Dublin 2 (01-767727). Mondays and Wednesdays: 7.45 to 9.45 p.m. Offers support and one-to-one counselling to enable people to cope with their grief.

Catholic Marriage Advisory Council, 35 Harcourt Street, Dublin 2 (01-780866). Local branches listed (with opening hours) under **Marriage Counselling** in the telephone directories or see church porch notice-board.

Catholic Protection & Rescue Society of Ireland, 30 South Anne Street, Dublin 2 (01-779664). Help for single parents.

Cherish, 2 Lower Pembroke Street, Dublin 2 (01-682744). Counselling and help for single mothers, including self-help group.

Challenge, Sion House, Sion Road, Kilkenny (056-21653/61210). Provides counselling and support services for single parents and their families; also foster care, adoption and befriending services.

213

Clanwilliam Institute, 18 Clanwilliam Terrace, Grand Canal Quay, Dublin 2 (01-761363/762881). Personal, marriage and family consultants. Fees are on a sliding scale. Special consideration given to medical card holders. By appointment.

Divorce Action Group, P.O. Box 2384, Dublin 6 (01-504627). Pressure group for divorce.

Family Mediation Service, 5th Floor, Block 1, Irish Life Centre, Lower Abbey Street, Dublin 1 (01-728277). Free, Government-funded service. By appointment.

Family Mediator, Michael Williams, 14 Charleville Road, Dublin 6 (01-978402). By appointment.

Federation of Services for Unmarried Parents and their Children, 36 Upper Rathmines Road, Dublin 6 (01-964155). An umbrella organisation co-ordinating and informing all agencies and groups for unmarried parents and their children.

Gingerbread Ireland, Information Centre, top floor, 12 Wicklow Street, Dublin 2 (01-710291). Hours (weekdays): 10 a.m. to 5 p.m. Provides counselling and mediation (both by appointment), and legal assistance. New members' night: Thursdays, 8.30 p.m. Self-help group for lone parents, with a range of social activities for adults and children. For local branches, contact the Dublin centre or your local community information centre.

Irish Society for the Prevention of Cruelty to Children (ISPCC), Molesworth Street, Dublin 2 (01-760423).

ISPCC Family Centre, 80 Primrose Grove, Dublin 5 (01-472555).

ISPCC St Joseph's Day Nursery, Bray (01-860776).
ISPCC Rainbow Pre-School, 30 St Ronan's Park, Dublin 22 (01-570937).

Marriage Counselling Services, 24 Grafton Street, Dublin 2 (01-720341) and 23 Tuckey Street, Cork (021-277906). By appointment morning, afternoon and evening.

Morales Foreign Divorce Agency, 87 North Circular Road, Dublin 7 (01-388196).

National Association of Widows in Ireland, 12 Upper Ormond Quay, Dublin 7 (01-770977). Represents the interests and needs of widows; holds self-help groups for the recently bereaved.

National Social Service Board, 71 Lower Leeson Street, Dublin 2 (01-616422). Linked to community information centres throughout the country; produces regular information bulletins on social welfare, housing, new legislation etc.

One Plus, Single Parents' Information and Support Group, St Helena's Resource Centre, St Helena's Road, Finglas South, Dublin 11 (01-345407/343558).

PACT, Support and Counselling Services for Single Parents, 71 Brighton Road, Rathgar, Dublin 6 (01-906438). Interdenominational counselling for unmarried parents.

Parents Alone Resource Centre, Community Project, 325 Bunratty Road, Dublin 5 (01-481872).

Parents Under Stress, Carmichael House, North Brunswick Street, Dublin 7 (01-733500). Offers a service to parents who fear that family stress may lead them to child-battering.

Protestant Aid, 74 Upper Leeson Street, Dublin 2 (01-684298). Provides assistance for needy families.

Rape Crisis Centres, Counselling Service, 70 Lower Leeson Street, Dublin 2 (01-614911; after 5.30 p.m. and weekends 01-614564); Clonmel (052-24111); Cork (021-968086); Galway (091-64983); Waterford (051-73362).

Samaritans, 112 Marlborough Street, Dublin 1 (01-727700). Cork (021-271323); Ennis (065-29777); Galway (091-61222); Limerick (061-42111); Sligo (071-42011); Tralee (066-22566); Waterford (051-72114).

Separated Persons' Association, Carmichael House, North Brunswick Street, Dublin 7 (01-721233). Meetings on Mondays at 8.30 p.m. Branch in Cork.

St Vincent de Paul Society, Headquarters: 8 New Cabra Road, Dublin 7 (01-384164). Practical help for needy families and individuals. Ask your local community information centre or clergyman for local contacts.

Stepfamily, The National Stepfamily Association, 162 Tenison Road, Cambridge CB1 2DP (03-0223-460312).

Widowers' Association, c/o Joe Malone, 71 Coltry Avenue, Ballymun, Dublin 11 (01-475169).

Women's Aid, P.O. Box 791, Dublin 6 (01-961002). Twenty-four-hour service. Navan Women's Aid (046-22393). For hostels and shelters in Athlone, Bray, Cork, Drogheda, Galway and Northern Ireland ring Dublin Women's Aid. Also see HOSTELS/REFUGES below.

Health

Cura, 30 South Anne Street, Dublin 2 (01-710598). For branches throughout the country see telephone directories. Roman Catholic counselling for unplanned pregnancies.

Drug Treatment Centre Board, Drug Addiction Treatment Centre, Trinity Court, 30 Pearse Street, Dublin 2 (771122).

Dublin Well Woman Centre, 73 Lower Leeson Street, Dublin 2 (01-610083/610086) and 60 Eccles Street, Dublin 1 (01-302626/728051). Offers comprehensive health care for women and family planning advice.

Eastern Health Board, General Administration Headquarters, 1 James Street, Dublin 8 (01-537951).

Eastern Health Board, Community Care Headquarters, 138 Thomas Street, Dublin 8 (01-719222). Includes section for Refund Scheme for Medicines, Dental Services and Choice of Doctor Scheme.

Eastern Health Board Maternity Services, Park House, North Circular Road, Dublin 7 (01-303444).

Eastern Health Board Supplementary Welfare Section, Park House, North Circular Road, Dublin 7 (01-387122).

Family Planning Clinics, in most large towns; see telephone directories.

Voluntary Health Insurance, VHI House, 20 Lower Abbey Street, Dublin 1 (01-724499).

Housing

Focus Point, 14A Eustace Street, Dublin 2 (01-712555); administration (01-776421). Advice and lobbying group for homeless people.

Threshold, Housing Advice and Research Centre, Church Street, Dublin 7 (01-726311). Helps people with housing, landlord-tenant problems. Has a number of advice centres.

Hostels/Refuges

Athlone: Crisis Centre, Athlone (0902-74122).

Cork: Cuanlee, Kyrl's Quay, Cork (021-277594).

Dublin: Family Aid, Rathmines Road, Dublin 6 (01-961002); Regina Coeli Hostel, Morning Star Avenue, North Brunswick Street, Dublin 7 (01-723142); Missionary Sisters, 223 South Circular Road, Dublin 8 (01-540163); Haven House, Morning Star Avenue, North Brunswick Street, Dublin 7 (01-732279).

Galway: Waterside House, Galway (091-65985).

Limerick: Adapt House, Limerick (061-42354).

Legal and Courts

Coolock Community Law Centre, Northside Shopping Centre, Dublin 17 (01-477804/478692). Open weekdays by appointment. Provides legal aid and advice to local people who cannot afford a solicitor.

Circuit Court Family Office, Áras Uí Dhálaigh, Inns Quay, Dublin 7.

Citizens' Advice Bureau, 6 Camden Place, Cork (021-506922).

District Court Family Office, Dolphin House, East Essex Street, Dublin 2.

District Court Family Office, Courthouse, Washington Street, Cork.

FLAC (Free Legal Advice Centres), Administration Office, 49 South William Street, Dublin 2 (01-6794239). Also: 2 Tuckey Street, Cork; 15A Clanbrassil Street, Dundalk; Peadar O'Donnell Unemployed Centre, 19 Upper Dominick Street, Galway. There are approximately twenty Dublin suburban centres—for addresses ring Dublin 6794239.

Incorporated Law Society, Blackhall Place, Dublin 7 (01-710711).

Land Registry, Chancery Street, Dublin 7 (01-732233/725194).

The Law Society, 113 Chancery Lane, London WC2A 1PL (03-071-242-1222).

Legal Aid Board, 47 Upper Mount Street, Dublin 2 (01-615811/615774).

Legal Aid Board Law Centres, full-time centres: *Cork*: 24 North Mall, Cork (021-300365); 52 South Mall, Cork (021-275998); *Dublin*: 45 Lower Gardiner Street, Dublin 1 (01-787295); 9 Lower Ormond Quay, Dublin 1 (01-724133); Aston House, Aston Place, Dublin 2 (01-712177/712725); 517 Main Street, Tallaght (01-511519); *Galway*: 5 Mary Street, Galway (091-61650/65401); *Kerry*: 6 High Street, Tralee (066-26900); *Limerick*: Lower Mallow Street, Limerick (061-314599); *Sligo*: 1 Teeling Street, Sligo (071-61647); *Waterford*: 5 Catherine Street, Waterford (051-55814); *Westmeath*: Northgate Street, Athlone (0902-74694). Hours of opening: 10 a.m. to 12.30 p.m. and 2-4 p.m. In addition, there are part-time law centres in a number of places throughout the country. Ring one of the full-time centres for your nearest centre and its opening hours. Due to funding cutbacks these part-time centres, as well as the full-time ones, are apt to close from time to time to deal with the backlog of cases.

Registry of Deeds, Henrietta Street, Dublin 1 (01-733300).

Adoption

Adoption Advice Service, Barnardo's (Tuesdays, 2-6 p.m.) 244 Harold's Cross Road, Dublin 6 (01-960042).

Adoption Board, Hawkins House, Hawkins Street, Dublin 2 (01-715888).

Adoptive Parents' Association of Ireland, 17 Clyde Road, Dublin 4 (01-682685).

Children and Young People

ACT: Adolescent Confidential Telephone Service (by young people for young people), (01-740723/744133/729574). To advise on relationships, sexuality, conception, contraception, venereal disease and pregnancy.

Association for the Welfare of Children in Hospital, c/o Brookwood, Tubber, Lucan, Co. Dublin (01-889278/6281157). Can offer personal support if you have to travel with your child to hospital and can organise a visitor for your child if you are unable to visit.

Fostering Resource Group, Eastern Health Board, Park House, North Circular Road, Dublin 7 (01-387122).

Irish Foster Care Association, 60 Grangewood, Rathfarnham, Dublin 14 (01-944229). An association of foster parents, social workers, child-care workers and those with an interest in children in care. Offers information, support and mediation between foster parents and social workers. Monitors child-care legislation.

Irish Pre-School Playgroups Association, 19
Wicklow Street, Dublin 2 (01-719245). Branches at
Cork, Galway, Kilkenny and Limerick.

National Youth Council of Ireland, 3 Montague
Street, Dublin 2 (01-784122/784407). Promotes the
development of services for young people.

Parents of Children in Care, c/o Gingerbread, 12
Wicklow Street, Dublin 2.

General

Campaign to Separate Church and State, 112
Rialto Cottages, Dublin 8 (01-537732).

Centre Care, Dublin Diocesan Social Service Centre,
Cathedral Street, Dublin 1 (beside the Pro-Cathedral)
(01-745441). Open Mon.-Sat. 9 a.m. to 7 p.m. An
information and advice centre on a range of social
welfare, family, housing, taxation, emigration and
personal problems.

Council for the Status of Women, 64 Lower Mount
Street, Dublin 2 (01-615268/611791). National
representative body for over seventy women's
organisations. Lobbies Government on a wide range of
issues of concern to women.

Darndale Family Centre, 80 Primrose Grove,
Darndale, Dublin 17 (01-472219). Provides a wide range
of information on local and State services.

Employment Equality Agency, 36 Upper Mount
Street, Dublin 2 (01-605966). State-sponsored body,

working towards the elimination of discrimination between men and women in employment.

FÁS—The Training & Employment Authority, Head Office, Baggot Court, 27/33 Upper Baggot Street, Dublin 4 (01-685777). Local branches throughout the country.

FÁS—Employment Services Offices, O'Connell Bridge House, Dublin 2 (01-711544). Local offices in most towns.

FÁS—Job Search, Newtownmountkennedy, Co. Wicklow (01-810180).

Financial Information Service Centres (FISC), 87 Pembroke Road, Dublin 4 (01-682044). Also has local branches. Free advice on tax matters and family budgeting.

FIS—Family Income Supplement Section, Oisín House, 212-13 Pearse Street, Dublin 2 (01-779122).

Government Publications Sales Office, Sun Alliance House, Molesworth Street, Dublin 2 (01-710309).

Insurance Information Service, Russel House, Russel Court, Dublin 2 (01-782499).

Irish Council for Civil Liberties, c/o Tom Cooney, Law School, University College, Dublin 4.

PACE (Prisoners' Aid through Community Effort), 7 Upper Leeson Street, Dublin 2 (01-602870).

Salvation Army, Missing Persons' Department, 12-14 Eden Quay, Dublin 1 (01-743762). Traces missing people abroad.

Tallaght Welfare Society, Information Office, 1 Main Street, Tallaght, Co. Dublin (01-515911).

Women's Political Association, c/o The Council for the Status of Women, 64 Lower Mount Street, Dublin 2.

State Aid

Social Security Offices: unless otherwise stated in the text, enquiries about benefits and allowances mentioned in this book should be directed to The Department of Social Welfare, Phibsboro Tower, Dublin 7 (01-786444); for local offices see phone books. General information from Information Service, Department of Social Welfare, Áras Mhic Dhiarmada, Store Street, Dublin 1 (01-786466). Children's Allowances: Oisín House, 212-213 Pearse Street, Dublin 2 (01-711911). Pay-Related Benefit Section, Gandon House, Amiens Street, Dublin 1 (01-786444).

Social Services: See phone books under your local health board.

Appendix 2

Useful Reading

Characteristics of Children's Behavioural Disorders, J.M. Kauffman (Wiley, New York, 1981).

Divorce: The Child's Point of View, Yvette Walzak with Sheila Burns (Harper & Row, London, 1984).

Family Law in the Republic of Ireland, Third Edition, Alan Shatter (Wolfhound Press, Dublin, 1986).

Guides to Social Welfare Services (booklets and leaflets), available from the Information Section, The Department of Social Welfare, Áras Mhic Dhiarmada, Store Street, Dublin 1. (Published and updated annually.)

How It Feels When Parents Divorce, Jill Krementz (Gollancz, London, 1985).

NSSB Directory of National Voluntary Organisations, available from the National Social Services Board, 71 Lower Leeson Street, Dublin 2.

Nullity of Marriage in the Catholic Church, The Catholic Press and Information Office (Veritas, Dublin, 1986).

"Parent-Child Separation—Psychological Effects on the Child," M. Rutter, *Journal of Chartered Psychiatry,* 1971: Vol. 12, pp. 233-60.

Raw Energy, Leslie and Susannah Kenton (Century Arrow, London, 1986).

Second Chances, Judith S. Wallerstein and Sandra Blakeslee (Corgi, 1990).

Separation and Divorce Matters for Women, Dervla Browne (Attic Press, Dublin, 1989).

Social Welfare for Women, Sally Keogh and Ita Mangan (Attic Press, Dublin, 1989).

Surviving the Breakup: How Children and Parents Cope with Divorce, Judith S. Wallerstein and Joan Berlin Kelly (Grant McIntyre, 1986).

The Complete Natural Health Consultant, Michael van Straten (Ebury Press, London, 1987).

The Separation Survival Handbook, Helen Garlick (Penguin Books, 1989).

The Single File: How to live alone and like it, Deanna Maclaren (Sphere Books, London, 1983).

The Single Parent's Survival Guide, Sandra Sedgbeer and Caroline Buchanan (Thorsons, London, 1990).

Women and Poverty, Mary Daly (Attic Press, Dublin, 1989).

Appendix 3

Glossary of Legal Terms

Affidavit: a written statement on oath.

Affiliation: the assignment of a child born out of wedlock to its father, obliging him to maintain it.

Constructive desertion: to be deemed to have left the matrimonial home with just cause.

Custody: the right to the care and control of another, as a minor.

Dependent domicile: a minor who has the domicile of the parent with whom he or she resides.

Domicile: a person's legal place of residence.

Guardian of minors: one who has rights of another, as a minor.

Intestate: one who has died without having made a will.

Judicial Separation: legal separation of husband and wife which does not leave either party free to marry again.

Jurisdiction: legal authority; also: district over which any authority extends.

Nullity of marriage: a matrimonial suit instituted for the purpose of obtaining a decree declaring that a supposed marriage is null and void.

Putative father: the supposed or reputed father of a child born out of wedlock.

Testamentary guardian: a person appointed by deed or will to be guardian to a minor.

Testator: a person who makes a will.

Ward of Court: a minor who has been placed under the protection of the court which then assumes responsibility for all the major decisions relating to that child.

INDEX

231

Women Surviving
Studies in the History of Irish Women in the 19th and 20th centuries

Edited by

Maria Luddy and Cliona Murphy

This highly original collection of historical articles addresses aspects of women's history in nineteenth and early twentieth-century Ireland, including: nuns in society; paupers and prostitutes; the impact of international feminists on the Irish suffrage movement and women's contribution to post-Independence Irish politics.

POOLBEG

In Quiet Places
The Uncollected Stories, Letters and Critical Prose of Michael McLaverty

Edited with an Introduction by Sophia Hillam King

This collection provides a unique and fascinating insight into the mind and artistic development of one of Ireland's finest writers

POOLBEG

IRISH SAGAS
AND
FOLK TALES

Eileen O'Faoláin

Here is a classic collection of tales from the folklore of Ireland. It begins with the heroic sagas, the ancestral tales of men and gods — *The Children of Lir*, *The Fate of the Sons of Usnach*, and the magnificent *Cattle-Raid of Cooley* (the story of the Táin). Then comes the noble tales of Finn and the Fianna, Oisin in the Land of the Ever Young, and the Pursuit of Dermot and Grania. Finally there are the chimney-corner tales of the Little People — *The Black Thief*, *The Bird of the Golden Land,* and many others. Throughout the book, Eileen O'Faoláin maintains a fine command of beautiful, flowing language and captures the heart of Irish story-telling at its enchanting best.

POOLBEG

THE SECRET ARMY

J. Bowyer Bell

The Secret Army is the definitive work on the IRA. It provides an absorbing account of a movement which has had a profound effect on the shaping of the modern Irish state. J. Bowyer Bell, a specialist in the problems of unconventional war, terrorism, risk analysis and crisis management, has been a research scholar at Harvard and MIT and at the Institute of War and Peace Studies, Columbia University. He is now President of the International Analysis Centre in New York. He has written more than a dozen books, including *Assassin! The Theory and Practice of Political Violence* and *The Gun in Politics: An Analysis of Irish Political Conflict 1916-1986*.

POOLBEG

Terrible Beauty

Diana Norman

Constance Markievicz was the most remarkable Irish woman of her generation. Renouncing her Protestant Ascendancy upbringing, she threw herself wholeheartedly into the struggle for independence which dominated Irish politics in the first two decades of this century. A dedicated feminist, she campaigned for equality and suffrage for women, viewing these aspirations as part of the nationalist issue. An ardent socialist, she was committed, alongside Connolly and Larkin, to the cause of Labour and the freedom of workers.

Imprisoned several times by the British authorities and sentenced to death for her part in the Easter Rising of 1916, Constance Markievicz went on to win election in 1918 as the first woman member of parliament, and then the world's first woman Minister of Labour in the first Dáil Éireann. Her courageous action and politial achievements earned her the respect and affection of ordinary Irish men and women.

Diana Norman has written a warm and sympathetic biography, in which her subject's personality is shaped by the threefold influences of resurgent nationalism, feminism and socialism. Believing her to have received less than her full due from previous biographers, Diana Norman here restores Constance Markievicz to a pre-eminent position not just in Irish history but in the history of women in the twentieth century.

POOLBEG

The Poolbeg
Golden Treasury of
Well Loved Poems

Edited by Sean McMahon

The *Poolbeg Golden Treasury* is a delightful anthology of everyone's favourite poems. There are pieces to be recited aloud, others to be savoured in solitude. The book brims over with patriotic odes, romantic lyrics, stirring ballads, poems evoking a far-off time and place. It ties together the strands of different traditions into a garland of well-loved verse.

POOLBEG